MISSION *Possible!*

Volume Two

Insight Publishing Company
Sevierville, Tennessee

Published by Insight Publishing Company
P.O. Box 4189
Sevierville, Tennessee 37864

Printed in the United States of America

ISBN 1-885640-85-4

MISSION *Possible!*

Radio Program

The exciting chapters in this volume of
Mission Possible! were taken from interviews
recorded for the *Mission Possible! Radio Program*
heard on select radio stations across America.

Each contributor was interviewed by
David E. Wright and *Alexandria Altman*.

Contents

Foreword

"Two heads are better than one." If this time-tested saying is really true, then why not add more heads? Some say that too many cooks can spoil the broth, but when it comes to collecting wisdom about how to succeed in life, you really can't get too much advice, especially from those whose lives bear clear evidence that their strategies work!

If you are like most people, you may find it hard to digest and implement the lessons of a dozen books from a dozen unique authors. Wouldn't it be great to simply sit down and chat with a group of leaders who have proven that anyone can overcome life's obstacles and to hear the simple, unadulterated truths behind their life lessons? Now you can.

Mission Possible! should be required reading for anyone wanting to grow and succeed. Regardless of which life area you are trying to impact, these twelve personalities offer hope, encouragement, and practical advice that really works! You will feel as if they are all talking right to you, giving you a leg up on the competition and a pat on the back to help you succeed.

Don't miss a chapter of this exciting edition of *Mission Possible!*, and watch for new releases coming soon to a bookstore near you.

Chapter 1

Dr. John Gray

16 - celebrate Monk

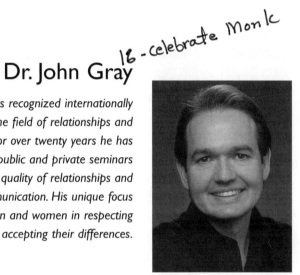

John Gray, Ph.D., is recognized internationally as a leader in the field of relationships and personal growth. For over twenty years he has conducted public and private seminars to enrich the quality of relationships and improve communication. His unique focus is assisting men and women in respecting and accepting their differences.

The Interview

David E. Wright (Wright)

Today we're talking with Dr. John Gray, author of twelve best-selling books, including the modern classic *Men Are from Mars, Women Are from Venus,* which has sold more than eleven million copies worldwide. An internationally recognized expert in the fields of communications, relationships, and personal growth, John Gray's unique focus is assisting men and women in understanding, respecting, and appreciating their differences. Dr. Gray, to continue your biography would take up the entire half hour, so let me simply say, Dr. John Gray, welcome to *Mission Possible!*.

Dr. John Gray (Gray)

Why, thank you. I'm happy to be with you.

Wright

Dr. Gray, you've appeared on *Good Morning America, The Today Show, The View, Politically Incorrect, Larry King Live, Regis and Kathy Lee, Roseanne, The Charles Grodin Show, Oprah,* and your work has been the focus of a two-hour *Barbara Walters Special* on ABC. With all this attention from the media, are people fascinated by the differences between sexes or do they really want to know how they can build and maintain better relationships?

Gray

I think the underlying current is that we're in a crisis time. We've been in a crisis time of change. With a greater influx of women into the workplace in the last sixty years, the economic balance between men and women has changed. When women are no longer dependent as much on men for financial security, a woman's expectations change in her relationship.

In 1969 when no-fault divorce was instituted by the government, divorce statistics went from ten to fifty percent. It was women saying, "Hey, I'm not going to put up with this if I don't have to." So women's expectations have gotten higher; they want more in relationships, and I think men have followed along and have basically said, "We want more too," in a different way. It's really women who motivated this change that sort of upset the cart, saying, "We want more and we deserve more." They're looking for companionship and communication; they're looking for empathy, more romance. It's suddenly as if they have more choice. They are saying, "Okay, I want something better." Men are trying to figure out what that is.

The question in men's minds has always been, "What do women want?" as if we really are from different planets. We don't really understand each other that well, and never in history have we expected so much from relationships. Unless we have a greater understanding of what each other wants, we can't achieve that.

I think men want to make women happy, and women want to make men happy. We want to have happy, loving, romantic, passionate relationships. The popularity of the book is that for many people the book fulfills the promise to give them the missing insight into the differences between men and women. Therefore, conflict becomes less in relationships, and it becomes easier. We're able to create more of the connection and the passion that we want to create because we know what we're doing.

Wright

Do you get a lot of feedback from the sexes?

Gray

I've gotten huge feedback. It's the biggest-selling book in the world—that's one feedback. People read this book and say, "Oh, gosh, I want my friends to read this book; this has helped me so much." The basic feedback is like this: "You know, I thought we were just too different to make this relationship work. When I read the book I realized the differences are inherent, that probably anyone I meet will have some of the qualities, so let me try to work it out with my partner. Now that I have a more positive understanding of the differences, I realize that I can manage them."

Let me give you an example. One of the ways that men and women are different is that we cope with stress differently. Men more often cope with the stress of the day by wanting to come home and not talk about the day. They just want to watch TV or read a magazine or do something fun. A woman will often come home and start talking about the day. She wonders, Why doesn't he want to talk about the day? She'll ask him questions and he'll give real short answers. She feels as if he doesn't want to talk to her, and she'll take it personally. That's the whole key to this. When we take our partner's differences personally, then we create problems, because he's basically just a guy not wanting to talk much and just trying to forget the day, and she's a woman wanting to talk about the day and remember the day. She thinks something's wrong with their relationship, that they have a problem with their relationship if he doesn't want to talk. With the understanding of men, she can realize, "Oh, that's what he needs." Just like she needs to talk, he needs to not talk.

So how does she solve that problem? One way is that she calls up a girlfriend and talks to her because she wants to talk, instead of expecting him to become like a woman. Another technique is to say, "Okay, let me just wait until he's out of the cave and then talk." She needs to let him know that it means a lot to her to talk, but she knows he doesn't want to talk that much, and that's okay; but when they do talk, she needs his undivided, full attention. Would he give her his undivided, full attention? If she asks for it, he'll do it.

Most men don't realize why a person would want to just talk. He doesn't see the point in it. He's not motivated to listen. When she talks about problems, he'll start giving solutions like it's some kind of problem-solving session, and that's not what she's looking for. After a while he says, "Why bother listening when she doesn't want to hear what I have to say?" He tunes out and doesn't want to listen to anything she's saying.

Now all of that is just a spin-off of one basic misunderstanding. So once you get back to the misunderstanding and correct it, then you have a much greater capacity and awareness and ability to have a mutually supportive relationship.

Alexandria Altman (Altman)

I hear those complaints about women all the time, and vice versa. So I guess we're coming to a meeting of the minds here. Dr. Gray, could you tell our audience about your latest book, *Practical Miracles for Mars and Venus,* specifically how it relates to our ability to make changes and sustain them in our lives?

Gray

That is the key to this book—making changes that we want to make. So many times we'd like to change things, but we don't even put any energy into it because we don't know how and we don't think it's possible.

Let's say you're in a marriage and it's been fifteen years and you just don't feel those passionate feelings towards each other. Generally, at that point, you say, "Well, that's what happens after fifteen years," and you give up. If you give up and you think it's not possible, then clearly you're right—it's not possible and it won't happen. If you restore your desire for the passion and for those wonderful loving feelings again, and make it your goal, you can achieve it. You first have to make it your goal, so that's the first principle. In this book I talk about Nine Guiding Principles for practical miracles. A practical miracle is making a change happen that you didn't think was possible. In this case, one of those practical miracles would be to bring back the passion to your marriage or relationship.

The first principle is, *Believe as if miracles are possible.* As if miracles are possible—it doesn't mean for certain that you know. As long as you're open-minded that it might be possible, change can happen. If you're not open-minded that it's possible or that it might be possible, it's not going to happen. You'll stay in the same rut, and things will just get worse and worse. Life needs to be a constant movement towards more. If it's not moving towards more, then it automatically moves towards less. You can't just hold life in the same place. It's either moving towards more, or it's moving towards less. You have to find out how to create more in different areas of your life. If the passion is gone, then you need to find out how to bring back more passion. If there's not peace of mind, then you need to find out how to bring in more peace of mind. If you're finding yourself getting sick, then you need to find out how to bring in more health.

These are the issues this book deals with—success, personal well-being, and, of course, our emotional relationships.

Wright

I was fascinated by your Nine Guiding Principles, especially numbers three, four, and eight. Three is, *Learn as if you are a beginner;* four is, *Love as if it were the first time;* and eight is, *Talk to God as if you're really being heard.* How did you come up with these pearls of wisdom?

Gray

Each of these Nine Guiding Principles I find to be present when miraculous things happen in people's lives. Let me give you some examples. I'm going to use these examples because they're more miraculous, but they're just like any other change you want to create in your life. I took the principles of this book and taught them to a group of twenty-five cancer victims in San Francisco. Three nights a week they would practice the techniques. In three months, fifteen of these cancer victims went into complete remission and are very, very healthy right now. These are people who were at stage three, stage four cancer. That means that the doctors had basically given up on them or had told them the disease was accelerating and it was time to go to hospice. Most of these people were on their way to hospice, preparing to die, and we said, "How about this for a last step?" and they volunteered. Five of the people died, fifteen are completely healthy now (gone into remission), and the other five stabilized and are slowly getting better.

This is miraculous. Everybody's eyebrows go up when they see that. These people are eternally grateful for what they learned, and what they learned to do was simply make some attitude adjustment in their lives. Doctors can help us, medicines can help us, natural medicines can help us, but if we don't have the attitude to support the healing, we're blocking our body from doing what it can do. So it's miraculous when the body heals itself.

Prior to this study, I had been working with cancer patients, trying to discern why it is that some people go into remission and become healthy again, and other people don't. Not just with that sickness, but with other sicknesses. I also saw the same situation in relationships—why is it that some couples make progress in their marriage and others don't? Again, I found that dramatic changes can occur when certain attitudes are present. The first attitude is, you have to believe it's possible. You have to be motivated to make the change. That's the first principle: Believe as if miracles are possible.

We'll skip to the third principle, David, since you like that one: Learn as if you're a beginner. In our study, in all cases where people had experienced a recovery, they were always learning something new. So it isn't so much what you learn that causes healing or transformation, but it is the act of putting yourself in a situation where you don't think you're the expert, but you're learning from someone else and you're on a learning curve. That involvement where you're learning something new creates a stimulation of hormones, a stimulation of endorphins. It is very healing and generates a positive sense of well-being, just the fact that you're being stimulated by something new and you're learning something new. Recent research has even proven that when you learn or experience something new, it actually grows brain cells. In the past we thought that we couldn't grow brain cells and that they were dying as we got older. Now it has been proven that having new experiences and learning new things actually grows new brain cells, which is, of course, growth. Instead of going downhill, we're going uphill.

Another principle you mentioned from the list is, Love as if for the first time. This is key to healing. When people get cancer or have a really big problem, often it's at that point that they're brought back to what's really important in life, and they realize life is short, life is temporary. They ask themselves, "Why am I putting up all these walls of resistance to people in my family or people that I've been a friend with or to my spouse or my children? Let me forgive them. Let the past be the past, and let me be in present time and make use of the time I have left." What they find is a willingness to say, "I love you," a willingness to find forgiveness again. This is what we saw happen in America with the crisis of the attack on the Trade Towers. We've been attacked, we've experienced real, tragic loss, and suddenly people are coming together, finding forgiveness for each other. Let the past be the past; let's all connect again.

So finding forgiveness, to be able to love as if for the first time, is key to creating miraculous change in our lives. Generally, we wait until tragedy sets in before we're willing to make these changes. What I'm pointing out is, don't wait for a tragedy to set in for a really big miracle to happen. Do it every day so that little miracles are happening, so you don't need the big miracles to save your life or save your business or overcome depression or anxiety.

These same principles help people overcome all the emotional blocks. I spent thirty years helping people overcome depression and anxiety with these same attitudinal changes. They had to first believe as if it were possible. But how do you get a person who's depressed or anxious to believe what's possible? There are techniques for this. For example, the first technique I would have you do if you are depressed or anxious is to sit down and look at what you want to happen. Even if you think it's not possible, what would you want to happen? You have to work with people to get to that place. They won't even give themselves permission to say, "I want to have a loving relationship with my spouse." They're so into believing that it's not possible, but you have to bring them back to how they felt in the beginning of the relationship and what their goals and ambitions were. They have to come back to the innocence that they used to have and find out what motivated them at that time, and then they start awakening what we'll call the endorphins of prosperity, abundance, and good fortune. That's how you get awakened, but you have to get in touch with what you want to happen.

Nothing happens unless you want it, and there are exercises for that. For anybody listening to or reading this interview, one of the first things you can do is sit down and write out your goals—twenty or thirty goals, not just three. You have to be prolific—stimulate, stimulate. Write down lots of what you know you want, and then ask yourself, What else do I want? One of the other techniques is the "what if" technique. Imagine you had all the money you'd ever need.

What would you do? Imagine that anything is possible. What would you want to do? Imagine that your partner totally loves you and forgives you all your mistakes, and you are able to forgive your partner. What would you say to him or her? What would you want? What would you need? We have to create an opening for us to feel our wants, our needs, and our wishes. This stimulates the actual physiological state that supports the psychological state that can create miracles.

Altman

Dr. Gray, in the event of a person having a major stroke, would that be the same as the cancer victim?

Gray

Yes, I've helped people with strokes as well. I've seen a person whom the doctors told that if he regained movement of his arm, it would be six to nine months, but he did it in a matter of weeks—he regained full movement. I'm just telling you my experiences here. I'm not saying anybody can do this, but I do know that the body is designed to heal itself when there's trauma or stress. We're not invincible. All human beings get sick, hurt, bruised, and damaged, and we mistreat ourselves. But if we stop mistreating ourselves, or stop being damaged, in a sense, then the body can recuperate.

For example, if you hit yourself on the head with a hammer, you're going to get a headache. If you do these techniques, your headache will go away. But if you then hit yourself with a hammer again, that headache comes back. We have to change habits in our lives. That's why a part of this book is also for health. I talk about some very small but important changes to make in our diet. There are certain things in our diet which block the body from healing itself. I always bring the body into it, because for any change you want to create, the body's involved in it. You have the physiological state that supports psychological change. One of the reasons that children are so much more flexible, can make changes, can grow and heal so much faster than adults is that third principle—they're learning as if they're beginners. On a physiological level, their body is naturally hydrated; they're about seventy percent water. But the average seventy-year-old is only thirty percent water. Hydration is a very big part of making changes. Whether health changes or psychological changes, your body has to have enough water to be flexible, literally to be fluid; and, of course, the most important thing is to remove the toxins that are caused by abuse or stress. Most people that I encounter are dehydrated. They may not be severely dehydrated, but they're dehydrated. You can look at their cells under a microscope and see that their cells are clumped together, as opposed to a healthy person's. The cells of a very *Water* healthy person are surrounded by water, by liquid. That's what is required to be healthy and resilient.

There's a study going on at Harvard right now of people who are over a hundred and healthy. They are finding that the number one reason these people are healthy is the attitude they have about *attitude* life. It has nothing to do with their diet, or whatever; it's their attitude. Their attitude is one that is resilient. They're able to bounce back from negativity in a positive way. They're affected by negativity like anybody else, but they're able to bounce back. The psychological term is "reframe"—to put it in a positive perspective. Like with the terrorist attack on America, we can live in fear right now or we can acknowledge what's happened and we can reframe it, we can bounce back and be resilient with more positive attitudes. One attitude is, although this is a tragedy, something good will come from it. Already a lot of good is coming from it: an awakening in America's consciousness of what's really, really important, a valuing once again of the middle-class aspect of America, and a valuing of masculinity—those firefighters going in and risking their lives. The whole valuation of masculinity has gone up.

There's a reestablishment of what's important in life. People are going back to the basic values of life. A bigger perspective is to recognize that in all of our traumas throughout life, if we know how to heal ourselves, we always grow and get stronger. I know this with absolute certainty as a counselor and someone who has personally gone through many personal tragedies in my own life. I've always grown stronger. The most obvious and simple example to understand is breaking bones. When you break a bone, if you reset it and put a cast on it to protect it, the body will heal itself and the bone will grow back stronger. We have to learn how to reset ourselves after a trauma.

One of the aspects is to forgive, to come back to how we felt prior to the trauma, to learn from it and grow from it. Again, this is what's happening right now. Everybody in America has a chance to look at what their issues are with security and realize that security never can really come from the outside. Our sense of security needs to come from within ourselves. We are empowered to create security by the way we live our lives. Many people are turning to spirituality, and that's a very healthy thing. They are finding their security now in spirituality, which is a very powerful way to feel secure. Then, no matter what happens outside of themselves, they have the security of knowing that they are supported.

Altman

Dr. Gray, in your book *Practical Miracles for Mars and Venus*, you state that being in an intimate relationship is like giving a million dollars to one person rather than one dollar to a million people. What a great thought that is! How often do you see this in a relationship?

Gray

I love that point; thanks for appreciating it. This is the value to us of being in a committed, monogamous relationship. We can live our life with friendship and love, and that's fine. That's a choice people can make. But there's something very special and also challenging to be able to give more to one person.

In one aspect of the book, I talk about stages of development of *Soul* a human being. The soul of a human being is always maturing, and we tend to mature in seven-year cycles. There's a major lesson to learn every seven years in life. If we keep learning our lessons, then that becomes a foundation on which to build the next floor. We're building a building. We build a foundation, then the first floor, the second floor, and the third floor. Many of us are over forty or fifty. We're on the sixth or seventh floor of the building, but we never built the foundation, or we never built the second floor. What's going to happen is, that building's going to start caving in on itself. We need to be able to strengthen all the floors.

What I'm talking about in the book is that message of intimacy, which I think is the fifth stage of life. This happens between ages twenty-eight and thirty-five and is the time when we develop the capacity to have an intimate relationship, a committed, monogamous relationship, where we're giving more to one person than to anyone else. It is a challenge to be able to do that. When we start giving more to one person, then we expect and demand more from them. When we don't get more from them, then we have a tendency to withhold our love. So that's a challenge. That prepares us, and we're able to overcome that challenge, to continue giving to this one person more than we give to others, even if he or she is not having a good day.

Then we're ready for the next challenge, which is at about age thirty-five to forty-two. This is the challenge of unconditional love, which is being able to give to our children in an unconditional way, or, if we don't have children, to give to society in an unconditional manner.

Wright

In chapter eight of your *Practical Miracles* book, you talk about life being a balancing act. Could this be a real cause for so much stress in our society?

Gray

I think that is the number one cause of stress in relationships—we become unbalanced. Let me give you an example of that. A man falls in love with his wife, and she's making him happy. As you know, when people fall in love, it's like, "I don't need anything; I've got this person in my life." What happens is, he becomes too dependent on one source of support. He tends to neglect and ignore the other areas of support in his life. He needs to take time for himself and support himself. He needs to take time for his friendships. He needs to take time for his work. He needs to take time for fun and play. He needs to take time to be emotionally vulnerable and depend on certain people for support—to learn and grow from them.

There are different needs that we have. I've defined all these basic human needs. Whenever we focus on one need more than the others, then we're living a lie. We're living the lie that "All I need is this person and I can be happy." Then we can't be happy. We won't be happy, because one person can't satisfy all our needs. That person may satisfy our need for intimacy, but we have other needs. What we tend to do is go into denial of what our other needs are. You can see all the crisis situations that are happening in America right now, and the war on terrorism is really a reflection of the problem we have in our relationship. The whole problem with the East right now, in terms of the terrorist attacks, is like a couple that are hating each other and are at war with each other. It's based upon an imbalance of dependence. We in America have become way too dependent on the Arabs for oil. First of all, we're not really dependent on them for oil. We have plenty of oil in America and in Alaska, but not forever. Nor do the Arabs have enough oil forever. But the bigger lie is, not only are we not dependent on the Arabs for oil, we just appear to be that way to keep the oil prices up. We have plenty of oil. My family's in the oil business. It's arbitrary how much oil we pull out of the ground.

The second lie is that we're dependent on oil for energy. We're not. We've got this idea of being overly dependent on oil, when really we're not. It's just that, unfortunately, people are making a lot of money from oil. They don't want to give up that domain. For example, BMW has already tested a hydrogen cell car that will run on hydrogen, which is basically water. This technology has been available for a long time. There's also a turbine that can be put in the ocean that will run indefinitely, generating electricity for all the cities in America.

There are tremendous alternative sources of energy that have been suppressed, not brought to the public's attention. There are even books written about it. Instead of putting two hundred billion dollars into new fighter planes, which is not going to solve any problems, we could take one hundred billion dollars or even a few billion dollars and put that into supporting alternative energy resources and start becoming energy autonomous.

What happens in any dysfunctional relationship—where there is violence, for example—there's always overdependence on one person and not enough autonomy. The first thing couples need to learn when they're fighting is to be more autonomous, learn to pull back and find their happiness within, find their security within. It's only when they are feeling independent and autonomous that they're truly able to have a successful, intimate relationship based on mutual interdependence.

What we have right now in our relationship in the world is interdependence; we've become a global economy. We have to make sure that we're also balanced and that we're being autonomous. In terms of energy, we're not balanced. The bottom line is that we're overly dependent on the East for oil; we send all this money to them and then, obviously, some of that money is used to fund terrorist activities. If the money wasn't going there, there would be no terrorists to start with.

Altman

Dr. Gray, my biggest surprise about you was the fact that you were a celibate Hindu monk. When you consider the choices you've made down through the years, has sex played an important role in your life?

Gray

I think sex has played a big role in my life. I'm a big believer in sex. I think sex is a terrific part of life. I think as we get older, it's a part of staying younger—younger in the sense of vibrant health. There's nothing wrong with getting older. I'm happy to get older, because older for me means wiser. It doesn't mean getting unhealthy, but for many people it does mean becoming unhealthy, so we tend to think of being younger as staying healthy and having vibrant energy.

One of the aspects of vibrant energy is that it comes through our sexuality. Sex is a big part of being a healthy adult. I have a tremendous interest in it because I've studied it quite a lot. When you give up sex for nine years (as a monk I'd given up sex for nine years), you become very aware of the power of sexual energy. You have to learn how to sublimate it. It's an energy that can be used in a variety of different ways. I was able to sublimate it through spiritual prayer and meditation and service. Certainly, it can be sublimated in that way. The worst thing is to have it be suppressed. But when you sublimate sexual energy, you still feel the sexual energy.

That's what people don't understand. As a monk, you don't stop feeling sexual energy, unless you've repressed it like many married couples do—they just repress it, and they stop feeling sexual energy. What you can do if you're going to be a monk is, you still feel the sexual energy, and you're able to transform it into spiritual energy that has its place. I would not recommend that lifestyle for anybody. It's not for everybody; it's certainly not for me anymore. But if you have an inclination in that direction, it's certainly a tremendous discipline to apply to your life for some period, or maybe for your whole life. But it's really not the route for everybody. Celibacy and being a monk is something of the past, because it used to be that in order to be a spiritual person you really had to leave town, go out to the desert or the mountain or whatever. That's a whole discussion that I have in the book.

Today we can have spirituality in our lives. We don't have to leave the world to find spirituality. We actually find the highest

Spiritual Life

spirituality by participating in life to the fullest and bringing in the values of love, compassion, peacefulness, understanding, negotiation, achievement, creativity, and intuition. These are all the qualities of a spiritual life at the highest level, which is to integrate the inner world and the outer world.

Wright

Today we've had the good fortune to be with Dr. John Gray, author of *Men Are from Mars, Women Are from Venus* and many other books. Dr. Gray, Alex and I really appreciate your talking to us.

Gray

It was my pleasure.

Dr. John Gray
www.marsvenus.com

Chapter 2

Carole Gill

For over twenty years, Carole Gill has focused solely on helping people in all walks of life reshape their personal vision of what's possible for them. As a professional speaker, trainer, and facilitator, her dynamic style allows us to unleash the power that we have within ourselves ... to become more effective communicators, collaborators, and team builders ... to grow to our fullest potential.

The Interview

David E. Wright (Wright)

Today we are talking to Carole Gill, owner and CEO of CRG Training and Consulting, Inc., a human resource development company. Carole and her team design and deliver training courses and workshops on topics such as personal growth, leadership and team development, customer service, and diversity awareness. Since 1999, Carole has served on the Board of Directors for the Tampa Bay Chapter of the National Association of Women Business Owners and is the president for 2001-2002. She is a member of the National Speakers Association and the American Society for

Training and Development. Carole Gill, welcome to *Mission Possible!*.

Carole Gill (Gill)

Thank you. It's my pleasure.

Alexandria Altman (Altman)

Welcome, Carole.

Gill

Hi there!

Wright

Carole, while preparing for this interview, I was interested in your essential business philosophy. If I can just quote you: "No matter how great your product or service might be, your employees can make or break the business." What do you mean?

Gill

Well, David, primarily people buy based on feelings. That's a proven fact in our world today. So in order to create an environment where your product and service can be marketed effectively, you need to be able to establish very strong positive business relationships, and that's all about people. You can have the greatest product in the world, but if your people don't know how to interact effectively with a potential client and meet the needs of that client, your product is probably not going to sell.

Wright

Is that the same as "relationship selling" that people are writing books about now?

Gill

It's part of it. It's focused on creating and maintaining positive business relationships with your clients and potential clients. It's about creating an atmosphere in your organization where the behavior is in sync with what you say your business philosophy is.

I've seen a lot of organizations out there that have identified company values and developed great vision statements that make me want to do business with them. Then I pick up the telephone and talk to customer service and determine very quickly that the employees haven't been educated on what those things mean. The behavior is out of sync with the values.

Relationship selling is based on the same concept, but to me it's more than just a sales process. It's about the entire picture that people see when they walk into your place of business, or talk with customer service on the phone. Are the people truly reflecting what you say you are as a business?

Wright

How much responsibility do you think the corporations have to get that message down to the people? Like you and others in our audience, I have suffered the same kind of pain, thinking I was dealing with a great company, only to find I've got someone on the other side of the telephone who couldn't care less about my problem.

Gill

You're right. Many times they don't have a clue what good customer service means. I think it's the organization's ultimate responsibility, and I think that the successful businesses in this century will be those that truly focus on the aspect of acting in a way that is in sync with what they say they are going to do. It's really about behavior. You can tell me how great you are, but when I work with you and it's a negative experience, or a less-than-helpful experience, all the words in the world aren't going to make a difference. Developing positive relationships is all about behavior.

Altman

Carole, you also said, "Individuals have the power within themselves to grow and exceed their own expectations." How would you create an environment to enable them to do this?

Gill

That's a really great question! I do this at every opportunity I have, whether in a training class or in an environment where I'm networking with other people. I think the number one factor is creating a safe environment where people feel comfortable expressing their needs, their feelings, and their opinions. That's a challenge, but it creates an environment where people are able to look at themselves and see more of themselves. Does that answer the question? It's really about self-discovery. When you create an environment where people are comfortable, they're more willing to look inside themselves and see how they fit in that environment.

Wright

I'm always interested when people talk about "safe environment." They use the word safe, but then in the definition, they talk about feelings. For example, you said that people want to express their feelings, and express their plans, and then they feel safe. What are you saying? Do they feel like they're not safe some way if they can't do that?

Gill

Sure. I think all of us walk around with the internal fear of saying something that will be construed as negative or be misunderstood. As a result, we try to conform to the environment that we're in. We all have these faces that we wear . . . some of us do it more than others, many of us are unaware that we are doing it. So to truly create an environment where people can reach their full potential, they need to be in a place where feelings are okay.

We've grown up in a world, especially in the last few years in corporate America, where you are not allowed to have feelings in the workplace. The problem is, we cannot turn our feelings off. They don't go away. We get angry, we get frustrated, and we get hurt. All of those things are very, very real. Creating a safe environment is about putting people in a place where it is okay to have feelings, then helping them understand how to deal with those feelings productively. It's important to recognize that feelings go with us wherever we go, and that each one of us has the ability to choose how we respond to those feelings. That's a safe environment.

Altman

So in the workplace, people feel, "When in Rome, do as the Romans"?

Gill

Exactly.

Wright

Several years ago I operated a company with a couple of hundred employees, and if you had told me at that time that there was a possibility that any of those employees would not have felt safe around my company, I would have just died. I would never have thought about it in those terms, but you are right. People do feel unsafe when they can't show their own feelings.

Gill

That's exactly right. And they feel like they will be contradicted or looked upon as being less than effective, whatever the case may be, if they don't agree with whatever the executive or supervisor or person in authority is saying.

Altman

And that kind of sets off a fear factor, and you start wondering if your job's at stake or if you misread someone. You just sort of internalize it and set up your own fear factor, right?

Gill

Fear is

Definitely. Fear is a very interesting thing. The word corresponds with "false evidence appearing real." We interpret what happens around us and send messages to our mind based on our own perceptions. Those perceptions create the fears we have. For example, I am extremely fearful of making cold calls in the sales environment. But the primary factor that is driving that fear is coming from within me, it's not coming from the person on the other end of the phone.

Wright

Right. How important is keeping a competitive edge in business, or in our personal lives, for that matter? And how is the best way to do it?

Gill

I think it is extremely important. I probably have a bit of a different focus on how to develop and maintain that competitive edge, David, than others do. I really feel strongly that competitive edge comes from being focused and being centered on what you are about. In order to truly be out there, to take the lead, to compete with others in our industries, we need to be focused on what it is we want to accomplish, what's the vision we want to create. I think it's critical to have a picture of where we want to go, then put the things in place in order to get there and hold fast to that.

Many times people and companies put great statements together to say where they want to be in the future. Then they hang it on a wall or put it in a drawer and forget about it. As a result, a year from now someone takes a look back at it and says, "Oh, yeah, we said we were going there." In order to keep the competitive advantage and the competitive edge, we need to have a clear vision of where we're going, and it has to be communicated throughout the entire organization in a way that people can internalize it, so the vision becomes part of them and what they believe in and what they stand for.

Altman

Carole, you've said that your best decision to date is deciding to live your life with intention. Tell us what you mean.

Gill

Well, it goes into that same philosophy that I just talked about. If I look at myself as a person, in order for me to live my life with intention, I have to know what it is I want to accomplish. I have to have a clear understanding about what my definition of success is. I can remember as a little girl hearing my dad make the comment to me over and over again, "I just want you to be successful." For many years my definition of being successful was making lots of money. But as I've grown and matured, I've come to recognize that success is not about money. For me, it's about a lot of things, but money is probably at the bottom of the totem pole. It's more about making a difference—walking away from any given situation that I'm in and feeling like I've been able to give something, to make it better than it was before. It's about stewardship, and it's about knowing who I am and acting in sync with my value system.

Wright

I wonder what we could do with the kids. I spend a lot of time with high school age kids, and it seems that none of them know what they want to do. They haven't given it much thought. They want to go to school, go on to college because their parents have said that they want them to go. But really, they have very little direction. What would you suggest schools do?

Gill

I would love to see programs in our middle and high school systems that enable teenagers to do some soul-searching, to discover their gifts and find out what they want to be when they grow up. That doesn't happen today. Here's a prime example: My boys are eighteen and twenty-one. Neither of them—even though Mom does what she does—really has a clear focus on where he wants to go. It's hard to identify that clearly when you're young, but it is important to put some goals in place. I think personal development in our school systems, focusing on helping the students know who they are, what they feel, and what is important to them, is really critical. We don't do that today.

Wright

Alex and I were talking to Brian Tracy just a few days ago, and he made the statement, "Not only are people changing jobs four, five, six times, they are actually changing careers." Do you think this may be a product of the lack of introspection in our younger years?

Gill

I think it has a great deal to do with it, and I believe our challenge is figuring out how to get that kind of education into the learning system that we have today. Our world has changed. Education has to change going forward as well. Reading, writing, and arithmetic are still important, but there's a whole lot more out there that needs to be focused on. Our children need to learn effective communication, interpersonal, and interaction skills in school. In a lot of my programs, I deal with adults who have never learned to get past the self-imposed limitations they've had since they were very young children. It's not part of our educational process.

Wright

You have been counseling, coaching, and consulting with people for years. Could you tell us some of the reasons experts tell us that most people—some say as many as eighty percent—drive to a place each morning that they don't want to be?

Gill

David, that is a wonderful question, and I'll tell you a little bit about my story, because I think it fits right in. I spent seventeen years in telecommunications with a very large corporation, and I would say for the last, oh, probably six or seven years of that seventeen, before I started my own company, I was one of those people. At the time, for me, I believed it was really what I had to do. In my mind, there was no other option. That was definitely a self-imposed limitation! When I see people who are doing this today, one of my biggest challenges and passions is to help them recognize that they do have choices. When you're in that mode, it's very hard to see what the choices are. As a single mom with two little boys, making seventy-five thousand a year, it was very difficult to look at that and say, "I'm not going to do this anymore."

Altman

Exactly. That would have been hard to walk away from.

Gill

On the other hand, when you're in an environment that is not in sync with what you believe in and what you value, your internal compass doesn't work properly. As a result, you get stressed out, burned out, and eventually get sick.

Stress has a huge impact on our ability to function. It happened to me. I ended up in the hospital with walking pneumonia and was unable to work for several weeks. I did a lot of soul-searching through that process, asking myself, "What am I doing? I'm working for an organization that doesn't act in a way I'm comfortable with, and I'm not happy doing what I'm doing. Why am I doing it?" That really started me on the journey of understanding that I had choices, and identifying what my limitations were that I had really imposed on myself.

Altman

So you got caught up in your own thoughts of what you were saying earlier, that you were very uncomfortable in your own environment, right?

Gill

Oh, definitely. It was very, very difficult being in a corporate environment, especially telecommunications, with everything that's happening today in our world. I went through four different jobs in a period of four years because of downsizing. I was really bouncing around just to keep a paycheck. I was a victim. I truly felt victimized. I felt that I had no control over my destiny, and when I got the wake-up call, which was really a series of events that occurred, I finally sat back and said, "You know, I am really tired of having someone else be in control of my destiny. I do have choices; they're not easy choices, and they have consequences. I need to understand what those are."

That was probably the most freeing experience that I have ever had in my life. And that's what put me where I am now.

Wright

We all know single mothers who should have statues erected in their honor, who try to raise a child or children, and try to make money. On the other hand, there is the money-driven family that has two people working, the husband and the wife, when it's really not that necessary. Staying home and taking care of the children . . . there are those who do not really have that option, and there are a lot of people who have the option but don't elect to do it that way just because of the money. So perhaps it works both ways.

Gill

I think everybody has to make choices based on their own needs and their own desires. In my Leadership Development program, one of the tools that I use is a Life Inventory. It helps people identify what their real priorities are, based on six different aspects of a Life Wheel, things like family life, mental development, financial and ethical beliefs, and so on. Through that process, a lot of times people discover they have goals in their Life Wheel that are definitely not in sync with their professional goals. The inventory helps them identify that maybe their ladder is leaning against the wrong wall right now, and maybe they are putting their focus in the wrong place.

In order to get to that point, we have to take the initiative to look at our personal lives, identify who we are, decide what's most important to us as individuals, then sync that up with our professional life, what we do. Who we are and what we do are not the same thing, but they do need to be in sync with each other, and our goals need to be in sync across each component of our lives.

Altman

Carole, with our *Mission Possible!* talk show and book, we are trying to encourage people in our audience to be better, live better, and be more fulfilled by listening to the examples of our guests. Is there anything or anyone in your life that has made a difference for you and helped you to be a better person?

Gill

There are so many people and things, it's hard to pick which one was most important. I think I'll go with two. First was a quote by William James, who was known as the father of psychology in some circles. James said, "The greatest discovery of my generation is that a human being can alter his life by altering his attitudes of mind." When I first saw that, I thought, Oh, yes, that's great . . . one of those wonderful platitudes written by somebody that hasn't lived in the real world. But the bottom line is, it's true. When I started my own self-discovery process, I realized that my attitudes were really creating a lot of negativity in my life. And it wasn't somebody else doing that to me, it was me doing it to myself!

The other person is my father. I grew up in a family of seven children. Dad is eighty-four now and has lived with us since my mother passed away three years ago. He has always been a great mentor for me, and still is. Watching what he did throughout his life and understanding why he made the choices that he did has helped me clarify my center and understand what my focus is. Now, being this close to him and seeing where he is in his older years, he helps me understand what I don't want to do by sharing some of the lessons that he's learned.

Wright

Along those same lines, the single greatest book I ever read in my life, with possibly the Bible being an exception, was *As a Man Thinketh* by James Allen. You can read it in just a few minutes, but it can literally change you forever.

Book

Gill

I agree. There's one program we use, in particular, that is three days, spread over a period of time. It's really focused on self-awareness, self-discovery, understanding who I am as a person, and how I can make myself better.

Wright

Do you use the Wheel of Life in your workshops?

Gill

Yes, I do.

Wright

Back many years ago, I was in a workshop in Houston, Texas, and someone advanced that theory. I looked at my Wheel, and it was running kind of lopsided.

Gill

A little cockeyed, huh?

Wright

I made a few changes after that workshop.

Gill

That's the key, that self-awareness. We don't take time in our busy lives to really think about it, until some life-changing event or catastrophe occurs. My passion is getting people to pay attention before there's a crisis.

Wright

What do you think makes up a great mentor, Carole? In other words, are there characteristics that mentors seem to have in common?

Gill

For me, yes, definitely. Mentors are people who, number one, have to be authentic. In order to be a truly effective mentor, they have to be comfortable with who they are, they have to have their own personal philosophy and be able to identify what that is, and they need to be comfortable sharing their experiences and knowledge with others without the fear of competition. I think that's a major characteristic for an effective mentor.

Another characteristic is that they can ask tough questions. The best mentors I have ever had, have been people who have challenged me to come up with my own ideas as opposed to giving me the answer. As a role model or a mentor for people, one of the things that I try hard to do is keep my opinions to myself and ask questions that will help the individual move in a direction that will make them more effective or answer the question that they have.

Wright

Would a mentor confront someone who they think may be going in the wrong direction?

Gill

I think it's not so much confrontation as questioning, "What do you think might happen if you choose that direction? What do you think the consequences might be?" and then allowing the individual to come up with the answer. It's more of a guided discussion, a facilitated discussion. If I was mentoring someone and I saw him or her moving in the wrong direction, I would probably generate that discussion.

Wright

I remember reading a book about mentoring, written by a female author, and she said that everyone needs someone in their life that rubs them the wrong way. She was saying that, like oysters with sand in their shells, people get irritated by others; however, in the final analysis, the irritation creates a beautiful pearl. I thought that was a great analogy.

Gill

It is a great analogy. And I definitely have been there in my life—on both sides.

Altman

Carole, most people are fascinated with the new TV shows about being a survivor. What has been the greatest comeback you have made from adversity in your career or life?

Gill

Well, again, there are many. I think the biggest challenge I had was more of a personal nature than of a professional nature. But those two things kind of fit together. Several years ago, I had my fill of trials and tribulations. My mother passed away, I experienced some severe physical problems and ended up in the hospital with back surgery, then was the victim of a drunk driver in a very horrendous car accident. This happened over a period of about six months. At the same time, my professional world was kind of coming apart. I was in a partnership with another individual. We realized that we were moving in different directions, and I made the decision to go off on my own. We had some very difficult discussions and negotiations around that process—it was similar to getting divorced!

Needless to say, my life was in total chaos. In years past, I probably would have laid my head down in the bed, pulled the covers up over my head, and said, "I'm done. I just can't take any more." I think that several things happened for me at that point in time. I got focused again on what I am really passionate about, what I believe in, and what I want to accomplish in this world. I have a very strong belief that I'm here for a reason. I don't know what that is, but I believe God has given me some gifts that I am supposed to be using. As a result of that belief and a very strong support system around me, I was able to put a lot of things behind me, deal with those feelings, and move forward.

Wright

I've been in several group counseling situations where most of the people, when they talk about adversity in their lives, come to several conclusions. One conclusion that seems to be in common is that they found out through all the grief, the anger, and the fear who really loved them.

Gill

I can definitely attest to that. What I dealt with at that time in my life was extremely difficult, but I wouldn't change a thing as a result of what I found on the other end of it.

Wright

When you consider the choices you have made down through the years, has faith played an important role in your life?

Gill

Faith is the thing that keeps me going every day. I have a very strong belief in the fact that there is a power greater than myself, and I am part of a picture that is being painted. I don't believe that each of us has a predetermined path. I think all of us make choices. But I do believe, as I've said before, God has given me some gifts, and it took me a long time—about thirty years of my life—to figure out what those gifts were. My passion, my mission is to be able to use those gifts in a way that helps other people tap into the potential that they have to really do better, to do more for themselves and for others around them. That faith is very strong.

Altman

Carole, if you could have a platform and tell our audience something you feel that would help or encourage them, what would you say?

Gill

Well, I think I would start with a little story that someone told me a while back about a man and his son. This gentleman was diligently working away trying to get a project completed, and he was responsible for his young son that day. The child was getting a little bit challenged with keeping himself occupied. The gentleman opened a magazine he had on his desk and pulled out a picture of the world and thought, "Well, this is good; it will take him a while to put this together." So he tore the picture up into little pieces. He put his young son on the floor with the puzzle pieces and a roll of tape and said, "Now your job is to put this puzzle of the world together. When you're finished, come back and we'll take a look at what you've done."

So the gentleman went back to his computer, thinking he would have a good thirty minutes or so to finish what he was doing. Within five minutes, the little boy came running back into the room with his wonderful picture of the world that he had put together. Needless to say the man was very surprised and shocked at how quickly his little boy could put together this picture of the world when he was really not familiar with what the world even looked like. So he asked his son, "How did you do that so quickly?" The young boy looked at him and said, "Daddy, it was simple. All I did was put the pieces of the man together on the other side and the world appeared."

Altman

How neat!

Gill

I don't know who told that story originally, but to me it holds a very strong message. We're all made up of pieces of a puzzle. If a piece of our puzzle is missing or it's not shaped properly, our world can't come together. It's just like the Life Wheel that won't turn if it's not balanced. The only way I can find out what's missing is to go inside of me. Looking outside for someone or something to make me whole is not the answer.

Altman

That's a neat concept.

Gill

It just really paints a picture of what I'm about.

Altman

That's wonderful.

Wright

This half hour has moved very quickly. Today we have been talking to Carole Gill, owner and CEO of CRG Training and Consulting, Inc., and we've also found that she's a very delightful person to talk to. Thank you so much, Carole, for being with us on *Mission Possible!*.

Gill

Thank you, David and Alexandria; I really appreciate it.

Altman

We definitely appreciate it. You were wonderful.

Carole Gill
CRG Training & Consulting, Inc.
10002 Princess Palm Ave., Suite 318
Tampa, FL 33619 USA
Telephone: 877-CRG-5566
carole@crg-hrdev.com
www.crg-hrdev.com

Chapter 3

Tom Hopkins

Tom Hopkins has proven again and again that strong people skills translate into sales success no matter what the product or service is or where it is being marketed. His own career is a living testament to those principles.

The Interview

David E. Wright (Wright)

We're talking today with Tom Hopkins, a legend in the sales training industry. Tom's credibility lies in his track record and the track records of the students he has trained over the years. He has personally trained over three million students on five continents. He has shared the stage with some of the great leaders of our time, including General Norman Schwarzkopf, former president George Bush and Barbara Bush, General Colin Powell, and Lady Margaret Thatcher. Tom has authored eight books, including *How to Master the Art of Selling* and *Selling for Dummies®*. His first book, *How to*

Master the Art of Selling, has sold over 1.3 million copies and has been translated into ten languages. Tom Hopkins, welcome to *Mission Possible!*.

Tom Hopkins (Hopkins)

Hi, David; it's nice to be back on your program.

Wright

Tom, you were one of the first people to make training available to the sales industry in a format that they could easily access. How did you get the idea?

Hopkins

I didn't really dream up the idea, David. This is what happened: The company that I worked for back in the '60s had management training for the salespeople. So when I became a branch manager for one of their offices, I found that if I could just have a person stay and do what I asked him to do in front of a buyer, they could help that buyer more easily say "Yes" to the buying decision. I found that many salespeople are not trained. They just use their normal personalities. What I tried to do was write the script for people to actually learn to say both on the telephone and in person, plus a closing technique, which is a way of helping a person give you the final agreement. These have to be learned, and I think we were the first ones to write a workbook where people at our seminars could actually take home the techniques and study them and let them become a natural part of them.

Wright

I used to have a friend who did some sales training, and he said he had the most trouble getting people to memorize scripts. He told me that they always said, "I don't want a canned speech." He reminded them that after memorizing it, it's no longer canned.

Hopkins

Exactly. A canned presentation, in my opinion, is one that was scripted by someone else; the person who's trying to deliver it really has to internalize it. That's why the repetition of what you say to people is so important. Almost everything we say, we have learned, in essence, through memorization. If someone says "Hello," we say "Hello," and if they say "Thank you," we say "You're welcome." So most of what we say we have learned through repetition anyway.

Wright

Do you find that it's better to let the person on the telephone put it in their own words, or do you believe in sticking with a script that's very, very strict?

Hopkins

I think you have to have flexibility, and it depends on your personality and your temperament. To learn to say something that's foreign to your normal personality is not comfortable. I think you have to take a proven script or phraseology and then tailor it to you. Again, I think there are certain words you don't say. I call these fear-producing words, and if these words are in the script, they need to be eliminated.

Wright

Many of your students down through the years have said that Tom Hopkins doesn't just teach, he inspires. What are they talking about?

Hopkins

I think inspiration or motivation is probably fifteen percent of what I do. I think people today really need to believe they can be somebody, believe they can do something important in their life. They know my background of not going to college, of actually quitting after ninety days. They know I'm not a formally educated person, and I started with nothing. I got into real estate and didn't even have a car. I built our business for eight years and became the top real estate salesperson in the United States, and then gave that career up. It is really scary to have such a wonderful career at the age of twenty-seven and say, "You know what? I'm just bagging it. I'm going to go out and start teaching people and open up a training company." It was a really scary process.

I try to teach people, David, that many times in life you've got to give up what you've got in order to get what you want, and it also means sometimes you have to take a risk and handle insecurity while you build your business.

Wright

I sat with you many, many years ago. I'm sure you won't remember it, but I had a real estate company that at that time was doing five million. I started using some of your products as well as programs of another man that I met at the same meeting. I took my business from five million to forty million in three years.

Hopkins

Wow! That's kind of what I live for today, David, to hear from people that have used our books or tapes and gone on to have a better life for themselves and their families. That's the payment for the teacher, when people take your ideas and have a better life because of using them.

Wright

It goes further than that. Many of the people who worked with me back in those years are now very prominent citizens and have great businesses of their own.

Hopkins

This is what I love to see.

Wright

Tom, down through the years there have been more books written, audio tapes produced, and seminars given on the subject of customer service than any other topic that I've heard of in the last ten years. Still, customer service seems to be at an all-time low. How do you tackle that problem with your program?

Hopkins

First of all, I try my best to impress upon the people that are coming to the program that the key to our whole country being as great as it is, is companies making a profit and us paying salaries and taxes to support our country.

Look at the lives of the great people in the past—for example, Howard Hughes, who died and was worth over six billion dollars; or Henry Ford, whose net worth was a few billion dollars when he died. Those are just two examples of people who realized that the key to our success and prosperity in the United States is this thing called service—giving service to a consumer. Henry Ford put an entire country on wheels, which was a service to humanity, and of course that's why his tremendous net worth was accomplished. Howard Hughes changed an industry of entertainment in Las Vegas, went on to build an airline, which was service, and of course all his research and development in the sciences was service. People need to open their minds to the fact that the company itself has to be service-oriented, and then people have to be taught.

There are basically two types of people in business. There are task-oriented people and there are service-oriented people. For example, if you go into a restaurant for dinner, there might be someone waiting on you who gets the job done. The task is taken care of, you get your dinner, you get fed, you're happy with the meal, and that's it. Or you might have a person who's not only task-oriented but service-oriented as well, who gives the "extra." They give the pleasantries. They give the follow-up. They give you the little things that waiters and waitresses do that make you feel so darned important and so happy you came in. Thus your tip is usually larger, and you walk out saying, "Boy, I'm going to bring people here! That was a great dining experience."

I think most people are more task-oriented. They get the job done, and they are excited and enthusiastic about the way they do it. I think the leaders of a company have to impart this to people: "Our company is going to beat the competition because we make every person feel so darned important, and we give more than people expect." I think that's a philosophy our company has actually tried to live by for over thirty years.

Wright

I remember the TV show *Cheers*—you go where everybody knows your name.

Hopkins

That's a great example of that type of attitude, where people just almost long to go back to being served by that company.

Wright

You're right. The amount of my tip is always in direct proportion to how I was treated personally.

Tom, how large a role does natural ability and charisma play in the selling profession?

Hopkins

I've always had a feeling that this was a myth, that to do well in sales you had to be the "natural-born salesperson." In fact, I'm finding over the years that people who are the natural-born, stereotypical image of a salesperson—aggressive, talkative, a control-type personality, which I label the "interesting extrovert"—gravitate naturally into sales, but the challenge with them is that they think they're so darned good that they don't become real students of technique or strategy. They just kind of rely on their glib wit and charm, but that can only take them so far. It's wonderful if you have a charismatic personality, but you must also become a master questioner, a master listener, where you really learn how to lead people nicely and warmly to agreement. If you combine a great personality and the strategies of "The Seven Fundamentals of Selling a Product or Service," you've got something very powerful. I believe even the "interested introvert," who's somewhat timid, somewhat shy, but loves the product and believes in it, and who can learn exactly what to say to the client, can far surpass—long-term, now—the success of an "interesting extrovert."

Wright

I've been in sales all my life and love it. I hear so many people say, "Gosh, I could never sell anything."

Hopkins

I hear that, too, and it's so sad, because people who don't believe they can do it are reliving a past bad situation where they got sold something they didn't like or they got taken advantage of. The selling profession itself, David, has gotten a black eye in some areas because of the lack of service or caring. I try at my seminars to teach people to get themselves out of the way and focus on the clients and how they can serve them and give them a tremendous product. I have people today, thirty years later, that I sold a home to, come to the seminar and say, "In 1969 you found us a home, and we're still living in it. Its value has gone up to $300,000, and we paid $18,500 for it." I just love hearing that, because those were probably the toughest people when I first met them. Of course, they love me now because I closed the sale!

Wright

I don't know if the statistics would be correct now, but many years ago I went to a sales seminar at a university. The seminar leader said of all the college graduates that year, eight percent of them would go into some sales field, but ten years later eighty percent of them would be in some sales field.

Hopkins

Selling has become an honorable profession. So many people don't want to get master's degrees and doctorates and become professionalists in a highly-skilled area. If they love people, find a good product, and work hard at the business, they'll build a referral business. They can financially set themselves up.

As I go around the country and meet on golf courses these successful people who own companies, I find that most of them started in the area of sales, gravitated into owning their own company, and built a successful operation that was based on their sales skills.

Wright

Right. I do a lot of talking to people about their discussions with heads of companies. I always tell them not to be afraid. If you're talking to the president, you're probably also talking to the most serious and best salesman in the entire company. Anything you can say related to sales would be music to his ears.

Tom, with our *Mission Possible!* talk show and book we're trying to encourage people in our audience to be better, live better, and be more fulfilled by listening to the examples of our guests. Is there anything or anyone in your life that has made a difference for you and helped you to be a better person?

Hopkins

Oh, definitely! There are people in different areas of my life. Most of my mentors that I had back when I started in sales have passed away, such as Og Mandino, Dr. Earl Nightingale, and Doug Edwards. These were my mentors in the '60s. I learned so much from them.

Financially, of course, most of my selling skills came from J. Douglas Edwards, who wrote the real book on the art of closing the sale. Actually, he never wrote a book, but he had his famous records. I took his records because they were so classic. His closing techniques are so fundamentally sound, David, that I bought the records from his estate and have put them on audiocassette because I feel that his wonderful fundamentals should never die. I believe he changed my life from a nineteen-year-old uneducated teenager, scared to death, with low self-image, to a top real estate agent. I totally believe that he was the man that changed my life.

Other people have done things in my life. Dr. Bill Bright of Campus Crusade for Christ changed my life by changing my spiritual life. I think Earl Nightingale with his famous record *The Strangest Secret* changed my ideas and attitude about how important it is to control my thinking and not allow negative thoughts to hold my mind. I've had a lot of wonderful mentors, and I try to take the things I've learned from them and package them in a way that people in this time and this culture can apply them and be better individuals.

Wright

You're talking about some of the men that I listened to all the time in my twenties. You're right. As I look back, even others like Bill Gove and Larry Wilson helped me in my thirties. I can almost look back to each decade and pick people like that.

Hopkins

Yes, myself included. That's why it's important for those listening to really search for people who can be mentors for them. Mentors can be company leaders who exemplify the type of person you'd like to be. I have a little saying: One of the keys to being successful is to find a person who is a success, then walk, talk, act, and believe like they do, and you will start to become them.

Wright

What do you think makes up a great mentor? In other words, are there characteristics that mentors seem to have in common?

Hopkins

I think so. First of all, a great mentor has the ability to take very important concepts and teach them in very simplistic ways—for example, my twelve words, "I must do the most productive thing possible at every given moment." That one little saying that I get salespeople to learn verbatim is the key to time planning.

We all have 86,400 seconds in a day. No one has any more, no one has any less. But at the end of the year, the person with the greatest income is the one who has the ability to take those 86,400 seconds and get more productivity than anyone else. That comes back to time planning, organization, and learning how to set priorities in your life.

I would say that great mentors have the skill to teach, and they exemplify what they teach. They talk their walk and then they walk it. They don't say "Set your goals" and then not have their own goals set. They have to live what they teach, be an example, and be a person that another person would like to emulate.

Wright

Even though this interview is going to come out in print, I don't want those twelve words to pass over our audience. Could you give them to us one more time?

Hopkins

I'd love to. This is a side note. I was twenty years of age and went to a seminar. The man teaching was very respected, and he said, "If you really want to be more successful, find out who the most successful person is that you know, then somehow find a way to take him to lunch. Pay for lunch and ask questions. Make notes of what he believes are the three things that have made him successful." So I did that. I found a very successful man who was gracious enough. I was only twenty, and he looked at me as a young kid who was trying to do something in his life. He said, "Young man, I'll give you these twelve words, and if you live by them, you'll have a very productive life." I was so sincere about wanting not so much to succeed but not to fail, that I took those twelve words as must-do things: "I must do the most productive thing possible at every given moment." That's not just when I feel like it, it's every moment saying, "What's the most productive thing?" And it doesn't just mean work. Work is only one-fourth of your life. You have your family that you have to do the most productive thing for. You have a business. You of course have your spiritual growth that can't be neglected. So it's setting priorities in all areas of your life.

Those twelve words are on a plaque in my office. My children have learned them. My grandchildren are now learning them. I really believe that little saying can mean so much if you start asking yourself all during the day, "Is this the most productive thing possible at this given moment?"

Wright

Like almost everything else, it's simple but not easy. Those are simple words, but for some people it's very difficult.

Hopkins

Yes, especially if they lack discipline. I find an awful lot of people who want success but have no discipline for punctuality, no discipline to do what they say they're going to, no discipline to follow through. If they don't have the discipline in their life, man, it's tough to be successful.

Wright

Most people are fascinated with the new television shows about being a survivor. What has been the greatest comeback that you've made from adversity in your career or in your life?

Hopkins

During my first six months in real estate, I only made one little sale. My money was almost gone, and I had no savings left. I was working straight commission, and I was scared to death. I wrote a check for my last hundred and fifty bucks to go see Mr. Edwards at his three-day closing course. The next year I busted my back, working seven days a week, probably fifteen hours a day. I was the first teenager in the United States to sell a million dollars worth of holdings. I would say my comeback was that I didn't quit, and fortunately it turned around when I learned what to say and how to handle people, and when I learned the seven fundamentals of selling.

Wright

As I listened to your answer, I was struck by something that probably means more to me than anything else you said. You took your last hundred and fifty dollars and paid for something that was going to make a change in your life. That was a leap of faith.

Hopkins

You said it! It really was. I always thank the young man who came into my office and told me about the program. He's the one that convinced me to spend the money, and I always will thank him for closing the sale with me spending that one hundred and fifty bucks to get educated.

Wright

When you consider the choices that you've made down through the years, has faith played an important role in your life?

Hopkins

Yes, definitely. For example, I mentioned earlier that my last year in real estate was almost ninety percent referrals. I was known throughout the city as the top real estate agent. The phone just rang off the hook with referrals. I gave that up to move to a state where I knew no one and opened up a business that no one had ever heard of. I jumped on an airplane and started doing seminars. It took a tremendous amount of faith.

That's why I try to teach people this little saying: "Today you're going to win if you realize you have to have faith, courage, and enthusiasm." You have to have faith in yourself, our country, our system, faith in God and His blessings, faith in the promises that He's made to us, faith in your own ability to be a good servant to your fellowman with your product or service. Then, of course, you do need courage to handle rejection, courage to go out and talk to people who may reject you today. Enthusiasm is something you have to work on, where you act excited, always happy about life. You radiate this and people gravitate to you. They want to be around you. They want to be like you. Faith plays a big part in my overall success.

Wright

I can vouch for your travels. I can remember back years ago you were the only one who was really going around to people like me in the real estate business, trying to get us to do some things that we needed to be doing.

Hopkins

I sure have loved teaching too.

Wright

Have you found that video has replaced audio as a learning tool?

Hopkins

I don't think it's replaced audio, but only because the automobile is such a great place to do two things at once—get to your destination, and train and motivate yourself with good training tapes. I think every car should be turned into a classroom, and you really can't do that with video. But video definitely has played a much greater role in training. I think a company that has a good video training system can put brand-new people through a training program before they develop bad habits, and they can do it right in their own office. We find that a lot of companies rely on video training today.

Wright

So actually they're two different things. I really learn better in my car. I travel with about ten hours of listening and I have, as you suggested many, many years ago, turned my automobile into a classroom. I have also found that within the context of the corporation, video is an invaluable tool.

Hopkins

Yes, it really is, especially if it's implemented and a facilitator in the company helps new people know exactly how to properly use it. You can't look at it like television where you just sit and watch. If you were asked what you watched last night on TV, you probably wouldn't be able to give us the main theme, the body, what was said, because you're usually not focused on retention. That's why it's important with video to focus, take notes, recite certain things that the video is saying you should say. It's really got to be interactive. It can't be just you sitting and watching.

Wright

I was working over in a southern state one time with a chain of national real estate franchises, and they had what I considered to be at that time the very best video training program that I had ever seen. I had been in the business for many, many years, and I was really impressed with the program. The whole thing cost $3,500. I started thinking about that and concluded it probably cost me a couple of hundred thousand.

Hopkins

Exactly. That's why companies are wise to realize, especially in these times, that getting their people focused, getting them back to basics, and getting them motivated and looking at the bright side of the future are so very important.

Wright

If you could have a platform and tell our audience something that you think would help them or encourage them, what would you say to them?

Hopkins

I think I would say that one of the keys to happiness is to practice living in the present moment. There are emotional handicaps that all of us have to work on. One of them is worrying about the future. Worry, I believe, is a fear of the unknown. It's also worrying about something that ninety percent of the time won't happen. I believe we need to control our thoughts as far as trying to stay in the present moment, not dwelling on the negativity of the past. Many people do that. They live with past failures, past hurts and pains, thus bringing negative emotions into the present. That's going to ruin the future. I think living in the present moment mentally, trying to control the negative thoughts that come into our minds, is probably one of the most important things people have to do on a conscious level.

Wright

That's excellent advice.

Tom, this has been a great thirty minutes, and I want you to know that I really appreciate it.

Hopkins

Thank you, David. It's always nice to be back with you. I hope the people listening and reading will try to apply some of the things that we discussed today. Application is the key to making it something that's natural and a part of them.

Wright

We have been talking today with Tom Hopkins, a legend in the sales training industry.

Tom, again, thank you so very much for appearing with us on *Mission Possible!*.

Hopkins

Thank you, David; all the best to you.

Tom Hopkins
www.tomhopkins.com

Chapter 4

Dr. Karlyn Black

Dr. Karlyn Black is a professional speaker, consultant, and trained Ph.D. health scientist, recognizing that "there are few things more valuable than the power to communicate." In addition to working one-on-one with clients, Karlyn (pron. "Car-lin") delivers presentations and workshops on effective communication, public health, and the environment. Using her technology skills and training as a graphic designer, for more than fourteen years Dr. Black has been helping businesses, agencies, organizations, and individuals communicate technical information in a way that is easily understood by virtually any audience. Dr. Black has taught classes at University of California, Davis and Berkeley. Her messages are "highly digestible," practical and real.

The Interview

David E. Wright (Wright)

Today we are talking to Dr. Karlyn Black, a professional trainer, consultant, and member of the National Speakers Association. In addition to working one-on-one with clients, Dr. Black delivers presentations and workshops on effective communications as well as health and environmental issues. Using her technology skills and training as a scientist, Dr. Black communicates technical information in a way that is easily understood by virtually everyone. Dr. Black has taught classes at the University of California, Davis and Berkeley. Dr. Black, welcome to *Mission Possible!*.

Dr. Karlyn Black (Black)
David, thank you. I'm very happy to be here.

Alexandria Altman (Altman)
Welcome, Dr. Black.

Black
Thank you very much.

Altman
By the way, you have a beautiful name, Karlyn Black.

Black
Thank you. I'm named after my grandfather Karl. When I turned out to be a girl, my parents needed to come up with something feminine.

Wright
Dr. Black, it seems as if new technologies come on the market every day. How does the average person decide when to switch to something entirely new?

Black
It can be a difficult choice for most of us. Fortunately or unfortunately, depending on our perspective, in this technologically-oriented world we live in, we are faced with these decisions just

about every day. It really comes down to why we are making the choice in the first place. Is it because we have a real need, or is it because of marketing pressure, or maybe even a feeling of control or prestige? The marketing folks out there are very good at putting new materials on the market and encouraging us to use them, in many cases, whether we actually need the new products or not. It's a real challenge to figure out what we should or shouldn't be doing.

In terms of choosing a new technology, you really have to ask yourself what your needs are. Are they business or are they personal? Are you choosing a new technology to perhaps improve marketing or communication? Are you looking to choose a technology for efficiency in doing what you do better? Or maybe you are choosing something new just because it's new. That's a perfectly acceptable reason too. It is important to recognize why you might be choosing a new technology.

In terms of when you might want to do that, you would tend to choose new technology when you have a very real need. If the technology you have right now is not working for you, you might want to change to something new. If the technology out there has improved so much that the technology you have is no longer compatible with other types of technology, you might change to something new. To stay in communication with others you may need to upgrade or purchase new technology, or you may even have a need to enhance or improve your business practices in some way that might require choosing something new.

Altman

Dr. Black, people say, "As soon as I buy this new TV or new computer and bring it home, it's like driving a car off the lot." Should people spend top dollar on new technology when it seems that after they get it home, even newer technology is coming out?

Black

That is very much a personal choice, in my opinion. Some people do have to purchase the "latest and greatest" to stay current in their field, to show they are on the cutting edge, or to maintain a technical advantage. But for most of us, and certainly for myself, the answer to that question is no.

Let's go back to some of the principles we've already talked about, such as choosing technology that fits your needs. In terms of upgrading or paying top dollar for the latest technology that is "hot off the assembly line," many times new technologies come on the market but don't provide significant benefits over what you are already using. You need to ask yourself, What are my technology needs? If the technology you are using fits those needs already, you need to ask yourself why you would move forward with something that's different from what you're already using, just because it is new, especially since it will likely cost you money.

The bottom line is pretty simple. On a personal basis, know what your needs are. Then ask yourself, Are my needs being met by my current technology? On a business basis it can be a bit more complicated. You still need to know what your needs are, but you also need to know what your employees' and clients' needs are, or may be in the future. You then have to ask, Is my current technology meeting the needs of my business, the activities I have or want in my business, the needs of my employees and clients, and the audience I would like to serve? If they are, great! If not, you may need to consider a change. In some cases you might want to consider paying top dollar for new technology if it will fit your needs better. For most of us, though, that isn't usually the case.

I would like to take a moment here to mention one other very important element to keep in mind when making these decisions. In many cases, the choices we make often come down to the people involved, not the technology itself. As humans we all have thoughts, attitudes, emotions, likes and dislikes, skills and talents. In some cases we have physical limitations. Until we have a handle on how the technology is or isn't meeting our human needs, we won't be able to make the decisions we have discussed here today. We should be using technology to improve the way we think and act, to enhance the way we conduct business, interact with customers or clients, go after new business, or simply stay in touch with family and friends.

In a nut shell, we should be using technology to do things in life that we want to do faster or better, not necessarily just more of. We need to make sure that the technology we have chosen is working for us, not against us. You may not need to pay top dollar to purchase something new or even to upgrade something you have, if what you've got already is working or older technology will still fit your needs.

Wright

I use the Internet daily in my business, and my provider has gone up and up in the upgrades in the last two or three years. It doesn't cost anything, so I go ahead and download their new editions of whatever it is, fearing that if I don't, something won't work in the future. But I have to admit that every time I upgrade, the changes are so insignificant that sometimes I feel as if the changes are only graphics. You mentioned graphics a while ago. Is that basically why they do it?

Black

Often times it is. There are really two reasons why upgrades would be provided on a commercial basis. The first is to make sure you have compatibility with other types of technology out there.

That's a functional, very real purpose for upgrading. That's often why an Internet service provider or Web site hosting company or any of these kinds of business activities might provide an upgrade for you for free.

The second is often to address customer service concerns, improve ease of use when you log on to do your Internet work, to enhance visual appeal, and so forth. These upgrades are typically provided as part of your service provider's marketing and customer satisfaction efforts. Since these upgrades don't cost you anything, it would be a good idea to go ahead and download them, especially if they are necessary to stay compatible.

Where you run into challenges in making this decision is when marketing professionals and business service providers make upgrades available that will cost you out of pocket. This is often the situation with application software or personal digital device technology providers. These kinds of upgrades often involve physical upgrades to your hardware or software. However, we're not just talking computers here; we're talking everyday kinds of things like telephone services or calendaring devices.

For example, you might currently be using an answering machine that has a cassette tape recording system or a paper-type calendar book. These may be working for you quite well, but because of marketing you feel you might need to switch to a digital recording device or digital calendaring system, maybe even a special voice mail service that you would have to actually purchase through the phone company or a third-party voice mail service. All these kinds of technology provide a way for someone to leave you a message or for you to keep track of appointments. However, they provide distinctly different services that have different costs associated with them. Each might fit your needs but probably in different ways. When it comes to upgrading, yes, you are going to want to take a look at what they are providing. If the upgrades are significant and increase your productivity or provide a service that you need, then it's worth spending that money.

I have a rule of thumb here that I think may be helpful. The rule of thumb in upgrading or purchasing new technology is to stay no more than "two clicks behind the curve." Basically, new technologies come out all of the time. Upgrades come out all of the time. That does not mean you should upgrade right at that moment. You may eventually need to upgrade, but I would suggest you wait until the second upgrade, possibly a third upgrade, comes out. Often times the new upgrades are functional but they have "technical bugs" in them. These can be annoying or distracting and in some cases interfere with your current technologies. They may be good products, but the manufacturers need to keep working to make them better. By the time the second upgrade or the second product line comes out, the technology may be much improved and may serve your needs even better.

In terms of personal as well as business productivity and functionality, I recommend you stay with what you have until you have a real need to change. In both my business and personal life I place great emphasis on functionality. When you decide to upgrade or even choose something new, I recommend you take a look at what's out there and pick something that is already proven. Often it won't be the most expensive or newest technology available.

Altman

Dr. Black, I get promotional letters almost every week promising to make my life easier, to allow me to work faster and increase my income. Are these things really true?

Black

Yes and no. Yes, they could be true if you use the technology in the way that it's designed and if the technology that you're choosing will actually meet some kind of need that you have. It's not true, if what they are promoting isn't necessary for you to do business or carry out activities in your personal life. You may be able to work faster and you may be able to increase your income, but only if you're using the technology correctly and only if the technology is filling a need or solving a problem that was holding you back from succeeding in the first place.

We often purchase technology because it's faster, it has more memory or graphics capability or higher-speed access to the Internet. We believe the marketing experts and become convinced that we need what the technology is offering. However, in many cases we don't understand that the factors limiting our productivity, success, income, Internet connectivity, and so forth, in our businesses and home environments may be unrelated to the technology we are considering; for example, access to the Internet. Purchasing a faster computer with high-speed modem doesn't help us access the Internet any faster if the limiting factor is the phone line that connects to our home or office.

The bottom line here is to really understand what the technology is offering you so that you can make an informed decision. It's important to remember when making these choices that you don't have to completely understand how the technology works to understand what the technology will do for you. You don't have to be a techno-whiz to make these decisions; you just have to be an informed consumer.

Wright

I bought some technology—I'm sure you're familiar with it—on my phone system through my carrier. On this particular item, you can hit the pound sign and a double-digit number and it will dial the person that just called you. As soon as the people in my office found out about this, my phone bill went up about a hundred dollars. If they couldn't catch the phone, they would hit that pound sign and the double-digit number, and my phone bill really went up. That was something that I didn't need at all.

Black

Absolutely. What a great example! You probably fell victim to a very clever marketing effort. It could be a useful tool that I'm sure the expert phone people out there have done a good job designing and making available for us. You may not have needed this technology in your business, and your staff certainly didn't understand when it was appropriate to use it. These kinds of choices are definitely something that you want to take a hard look at in your personal and your business practices. Just because the feature is out there doesn't mean it is something you necessarily want to incorporate into your life. You might not want to incorporate it for several reasons. One, you don't need it. Two, it may cost money you're not willing to spend in that area. Or three, it might actually cause a decrease in productivity and revenue in your personal or professional life, as in the example you just mentioned.

One way to approach the use of technology is to take a hard look at how it works and when it might be useful, and then make sure that people using it have the right training to understand how and when to use it. It is important to make sure you and your employees have the right information to be able to make informed decisions about when they would and wouldn't use it, especially if there is a dollar cost associated with it.

Wright

Everyone seems to be fascinated with the potential of computers to increase their business. After all of the dot-com failures, is the computer really the "knight in shining armor" that people are led to believe it is?

Black

Yes, it is—but let me tell you, David, not in the way some people think, and not if we think computers can replace essential human interactions. I think that was one of the fundamental mistakes some of the dot-com companies made. Computers have phenomenally changed our lives. Within my lifetime, we have gone from computers that filled a large room, if not whole buildings, that required special air-conditioning systems to handle all the heat they generated, that needed two or more persons to operate them, that used punch cards to collect data and took three days to give you an answer to your question, to completely portable laptop systems, PalmPilots™, and other personal assistants, digital media, and whole multimedia systems of unimaginable microscopic proportions that can process data and send messages around the world within milliseconds.

The Internet and the ability that we have to communicate globally within fractions of seconds are really quite amazing when you stop and think that many of our grandparents didn't even grow up with telephones. So in a sense, yes, computers are "knights in shining armor" when it comes to communication. They have allowed us to communicate faster and more efficiently then ever, under circumstances that we wouldn't have imagined years ago.

Wright

What you're really saying is that, informationally, that would be correct, but the downsides are sales techniques?

Black

Yes, some of the downsides would be sales techniques. Another downside would be the human interface, what we're expecting technology to do for us . . . what we're asking technology to replace in terms of human interaction and human behavior. It all comes at a cost. The simple presence of computers in everyday life often creates the expectation that we can do business instantly, over great distances, twenty-four hours a day, seven days a week, without fail or error. In some cases we may be able to do that. But just because it is possible, the question arises whether the expectation is reasonable and whether we should try to meet it.

Just because we can send e-mail messages almost instantaneously doesn't mean we, as human beings, can create the content of e-mails any more quickly or that the content will be any better. Just because we have technologies that allow us to communicate more quickly doesn't mean we're communicating any more effectively or efficiently. This is part of what I offer in my business when we talk about technical communications. For example, in working with scientists and other technical folks obviously trained in a different discipline, I have found that just because you give them the Internet or computer programs or the ability to make slide presentations on the fly doesn't mean you've given them any better skills to communicate. You may have given them tools, but unless they understand how to use those tools, unless they have training, unless they understand how people learn and what they think and feel under many different conditions, they still won't be effective in communicating their message. If we aren't careful in today's world, we can become enslaved by technology and its application in our everyday lives.

In response to the second part of your question, David, the answer is no. In that sense, the computer is not your "knight in shining armor." The expectations for business and personal performance that have been created by the existence of computers can cause a great deal of stress in our lives and may even lessen the quality of our lives in some ways.

Altman

Dr. Black, with our *Mission Possible!* talk show, we are trying to encourage people in our audience to be better, live better, and be more fulfilled by listening to the examples of our guests. Is there anything or anyone in your life that has made a difference for you and helped you to be a better person?

Black

Oh, yes, absolutely. The very first persons that made a difference in my life were, of course, my parents. They taught me to believe that I can do anything in life if I put my mind to it. They also taught me that it's not going to be easy, and that it will take time and hard work and good preparation. My parents were undoubtedly my first source of inspiration. They gave me my first lessons on life and gave me many of the skills and perspectives I have used to succeed in my life today.

There are a couple of other folks in my life who have definitely made a difference as well. I had a high school science teacher, Mr. Henderson. Mr. Henderson was also a farmer. He worked hard. He was structured, a very tough teacher, and a person of great moral fiber with high expectations, but he made science real for me. I fundamentally believe I went on to become a scientist because of him. If you stop and think about it even for only a second, so much of what we are, what life is, can be related to science in some fashion.

I had another high school teacher, Mr. Morden. Where Mr. Henderson was rigid, Mr. Morden was relaxed. But he was also driven and had great conviction for his discipline. He taught me that there are many ways to solve problems and that it is the thought process, the mechanics of taking on challenges and meeting them face-on, that are much more important than the ultimate outcome or results of taking that action. In other words, it's important to take some kind of action, do something, as long as you're moving forward. You can worry about whether it's perfectly right later.

Altman

That's a great answer.

Wright

That's good advice. It might interest our audience to know that there was a survey recently where people were asked to list the top five people who have made an impact on their lives, and well over eighty percent of those listed were teachers.

Black

It's very interesting to learn that. And in my case it's not surprising, because I went on to do things very much related to what they were able to teach me in school. It very much shaped who I am as a person and as a professional. I have to believe, and I do believe this: In our professional and personal lives, it's not only what we know, but who we surround ourselves with. We start out with these folks in our lives who make a difference and help us become who we are. As we go on to make choices—and we all make choices every day in our lives—we should choose those people to be in our lives who help and support us, those folks who are our greatest fans, who help us move forward in our adult lives.

Wright

When you began teaching at the University of California, did you find yourself emulating those two professors?

Black

Absolutely. Taking from those positive experiences the best of what I could, using the things that I learned to value, and keeping in mind the lessons that they taught me, I started my professional life with a solid foundation. As I gained experience and confidence, I added my own personality, style, and flavor to develop what I do as a professional today.

Wright

What do you think makes up a great mentor? In other words, are there characteristics that mentors seem to have in common?

Black

Yes, there are. I'm not an expert on mentors, but I will tell you from my personal experience that all of the mentors in my life have had high expectations. They had high expectations of themselves for success and high expectations of me as a student.

I had two other persons in my life that I would consider mentors. Dr. Chapple, my college chemistry professor, was one of the first female role models I had as a scientist. She had very high expectations of herself and of me as a scientist. And there was Dr. Bothun, my English literature professor. She didn't limit her expectations to me as a scientist; she expected that I should be able to write and communicate well too.

All mentors, in my experience, are very clear in what they expect. They also practice what they preach. In today's vernacular, or the way we say things today, we talk a lot about "walking the talk" and "practicing what we preach." Mentors do just that. It doesn't mean that they are perfect people, but it does mean that they do what they say. I believe that is an important characteristic for a mentor. They also find the extra time it takes to instruct and advise. It's not enough to be a good example; it's critical that mentors stop in their day, in that moment in time, and take the time and make the effort to instruct others or advise them as they go through their lives. Even when you fail, people who are mentors or role models are there for you. They don't abandon you. They are right along beside you, helping you come through that failure. We all fail; we're human. No one is perfect. These, in my experience, are important characteristics of a real mentor.

Altman

Dr. Black, let's change the subject for a minute. Have you ever thought of what you would be doing today if you had not chosen your present vocation? Or, to put it another way, could you be happy and fulfilled in another job?

Black

Oh, my goodness, yes! Actually, I have had many jobs and several vocations already. Many of us change roles as we mature, grow, and move along in our professional and personal lives. Inside all of us are numerous ambitions and skills, many talents, characteristics, and traits. These can all be used in many different applications, both personal and professional.

I've already had several changes in my life. I was born and raised in a very small town in the state of Alaska. I moved from a small rural environment to a highly populated metropolitan city environment, in what we called the Lower 48. Even though I was trained as a research scientist, I have successfully moved into communications and consulting and other social activities related to protecting human health and improving quality of life.

I have the desire to do other things in my life as well. I think it is possible for me to be happy in other vocations, to take on new life challenges, and to be successful, because I carry with me all of my life experiences, all of my life successes, as well as my failures. I routinely apply what I have learned from them in new settings. I use them to build on, much like a foundation for a home—brick by brick, experience by experience. They define who I am today. I expect to change career focuses probably one or two more times in my life.

Wright

Let me go back to the discussion we were having before Alex asked that question. You're the only person in many, many people who has said that it's not enough to be a mentor, it's not enough to be a good example. That's the first time I've ever heard that. Of course, I believe it. I think that you're right; that's one of the real characteristics of a mentor. They are proactive, big time.

Black

That is absolutely correct. I believe in order to make a difference in this world, in order to make a difference in someone's life, one must be involved, must take action, and as a consequence take responsibility for that action. That's how you move forward from where you are today. No matter how you measure success, it's whether you do or don't take action that makes a difference. All of us have that capacity to make a difference. But when some people succeed where others fail, it's because the people who succeed have been willing to step out and take some kind of action. To be a true mentor, in order to make a real difference, you have to be willing to be involved, to take action, and to move forward in some way.

Wright

A lot of people say they read biographies and autobiographies of great people and take strength from them. They look at them as mentors. However, all of the mentors in my life—those people who have impacted my life more than any others—were not only great examples, like Abraham Lincoln or Oscar Wilde, but they took an active role in my life. They took a specific interest in me personally.

Black

Absolutely. That has been my experience as well.

Wright

Most people are fascinated with the new TV shows about being a survivor. What has been the greatest comeback you have made from adversity in your career or life?

Black

I'm not really sure that I have one—a greatest comeback, if you will. Professionally and personally, I'm a slow, steady kind of person who consistently sets goals and tries very hard to meet them. As I meet them, I set new goals. But I have had a health scare or two in my life. In that sense, my greatest comeback would be on the health front. I am a pretty hard-working person, and in this fast-paced world we live in, I must confess that it has been a challenge for me to balance work and play. It's been a challenge for me to make the time to take care of myself on a personal basis. It caught up with me in my thirties when I was stricken with encephalitis and meningitis, an inflammation of the brain. I went from being able to run five miles a day to barely being able to climb the stairs.

I am okay now, but once you contemplate that kind of health restriction in your early thirties, when most of us have phenomenal energy, or even in your twenties or forties—really at any time—it is very much an eye-opening experience.

I came back from that health challenge with a renewed focus, an interest and a renewed commitment to do all of those things that I wanted to do in my life, the things that were on my list. I added a few new things too. What that health challenge did was make me take a hard look at how I was behaving in my life, how I was running my life on a daily basis, and what my priorities were. I had to decide whether the things that I was doing in my life were important to me, were the right things to be doing, or whether there were other things that I might take on to make a difference in the world.

Altman

Dr. Black, that leads to our next question. When you consider the choices you have made down through the years, has faith played an important role in your life?

Black

Absolutely. I believe that if I did not have faith, I would not be where I am in my life. I would not have all the goodness and success that we've talked about so easily today. Although it also came from hard work and dedication on the part of myself and all the others who supported me, faith played a role. I was raised Presbyterian as a child, and I fundamentally believe in (with this particular religion and faith) the Ten Commandments and how we should treat others and ourselves, in humanity and social behavior, responsibility, and right and wrong. But even more importantly, it's about faith, about believing in good and all things possible.

In fact, my beliefs and faith tie in nicely to the message you are sharing with your *Mission Possible!* series. I was interested in participating because I truly believe all things are possible. It comes from a faith in higher powers. For many people, that could be God. For others, it might be humanity or society itself. We have many examples of that throughout history in many different cultures. All of these examples have several things in common. These things include faith and a belief in how to treat others and how we should behave as persons in society. Faith has absolutely played a role in my ability to move forward and take on new challenges, to be equally, if not more, successful in life. For things to be possible, you have to have faith. You have to believe.

Wright

Dr. Black, with all the aftermath of September 11, church attendance is up significantly. As for patriotism, almost everyone has sold out of flags, and people are getting together in ways that they didn't before September 11. Has that had an impact on you or has it had an impact on your business?

Black

Yes; in fact, I think it has had an impact on all of us. In my case, it's given me a renewed faith, supporting the belief that there are good things in this world and that we can make a difference. Even though tragedy has happened, at every single setback—or bad thing, if you will—in my life and business, I take a hard look and say, "What good can come out of this?" Even though no one would ask for or want the tragedies that we have lived through in the last several months, or even historically, what they do for us is test the foundation upon which our beliefs are built. They remind us that we need to move forward and have faith. They encourage us to believe and come together as human beings, as functioning members of this society, and go on and make a difference.

Yes, it has made an impact, because it has reminded me that the things that I believe in are true and that people can make a difference. We can overcome these horrible things that occur in our life and go on to celebrate the good things that are out there for all of us if we dare to get involved.

Altman

Dr. Black, if you could have a platform and tell our audience something you think would help or encourage them, what would you say?

Black

The message I want to share to encourage our audience to succeed is very simple: Every day is a new day. That means every day is a new start. No matter what we have or haven't done in the past, when we get out of bed today, tomorrow, the day after, we get to decide how we are going to be and what we are going to do, starting on that new day.

In my experience, the biggest challenges we face in our lives truly come from within ourselves. These challenges come from believing that we can't effect change, when in reality we can; from insisting that we do things on our own; from believing that there is only one solution to a given problem, or that we can solve something overnight. These challenges result when we don't get involved, when we don't ask for help, from not working with others, and from competing for limited resources instead of going after new ones. We make challenges for ourselves when we blame other people for where we are in our lives if we aren't happy, or when we believe that difficult things are "someone else's problem." Once we realize this, we are more than halfway there to achieving success in our lives.

It is important to understand we can't do this alone. We need to work with others. In some cases, we need to ask for help. We need to recognize that, more often than not, there's more than one solution to every challenge that is out there, personal or professional, and understand that sometimes these things take time. We need to stop competing and start working together, to stop blaming others for successes or failures in our lives and move forward and believe in our ability to make a difference. Every day is a new day. I ask you and our readers then, "What are you going to do with yours?"

Wright

That is a good question. Can you believe we are out of time? We have been speaking with Dr. Karlyn Black, professional trainer, consultant, and member of National Speakers Association. Karlyn, thanks for joining us today. It was a pleasure speaking with you.

Black

You're welcome. It has been my pleasure.

Enviro-Tech Communications
P.O. Box 593
Folsom, California 95763 USA
Telephone: 916.502.0500
Fax: 530.672.1488
KBlack@EnviroTechCom.com

Chapter 5

Kevin Lust

Kevin Lust helps make people's lives easier. As a professional trainer, inspirational speaker, consultant, and coach, he shares his powerful "Lust Lessons" around the world, helping people and organizations find the smart ways to reach their goals and fulfill their missions.

The Interview

David E. Wright (Wright)

Today we are talking to Kevin Lust, a professional trainer, inspirational speaker, consultant, and coach. Kevin has a wealth of experience not only from his speaking and training business, but also from his career as a commercial and personal banker, director of personnel, and manager. He holds a bachelor of arts degree in business administration and is a member of the National Speakers Association. In his audio program *Financial Fitness: How to Budget Your Time, Your Money, and Your Life,* Kevin suggests common-sense, workable methods to realize success, even for the most disorganized, overcommitted lives. Kevin Lust, welcome to *Mission Possible!*.

Kevin Lust (Lust)

Thanks, David. It's great to be here.

Alexandria Altman (Altman)

Yes, Kevin, welcome.

Lust

Thank you, Alexandria.

Wright

Kevin, you have made more than fifteen hundred presentations in seventeen countries. Coming from my industry, booking speakers for years, that is quite an accomplishment. What do you think is your most compelling topic, the one that you think people need the most?

Lust

The topic to which people really respond the most is a program I do on how to maintain balance in your life. I call it "Enjoying the Tightrope: How to Maintain Balance and Still Reach Your Goals." I think that balance is the part people most often miss when talking about or striving for success. For many of the successful people that we hear about, we learn only about their success in their career, whether athletics, business, or whatever. However, when we dig a little deeper, we find that in other areas of their lives they might not be so successful.

When I speak on this topic, I do a little "CPR training"—only it's not CPR training as we usually think of it. In this case, it's career, personal, and relationship training. We need to be sure that when we're striving for success in any one of those areas, we pay careful attention to the other two as well. If we're most focused on our relationships at a given time, we can't let our personal lives suffer. When we're focused on our career, we can't ignore our relationships, and so on.

Wright

Is that topic more accepted by women than men?

Lust

I would say that today all people are recognizing the need for balancing each of the areas of their lives. I don't believe that this is gender specific. It might be true that there were more males that needed to be awakened to the notion of balance, based on our historic role-stereotype as stoic breadwinner, the caveman with the stick. But given that we hear so much today about people "taking stock of their lives," if we use that cliché, both genders are moving in the right direction.

Wright

The reason I asked the question, almost every conference that I have attended in the last fifteen years has offered a breakout session especially for women, titled "How to Balance Your Life and Career." I've always thought that to be strange, because men need that as much as women.

Lust

Absolutely. I suspect that females have recognized the need to attend to this earlier because, in many cases, their roles haven't changed at home, even while their roles were changing in the workplace. Women have been taking on greater and greater responsibilities at work, and we're seeing them move farther and farther into corporate hierarchies. At the same time, in many cases, they've still maintained the traditional roles of wife and mother at home. They have felt more compelled, I think, to maintain focus on both sides.

Altman

Kevin, we're superwomen now.

Lust

That's right, and you always have been.

Altman

Kevin, one of your topics, "Integrity Means Doing Your Best When No One Is Looking," caught my attention. Is there really much integrity left in the global corporate world today?

Lust

Of course. That we don't hear about it is the problem. Companies don't usually make the news for being moral and upright. Well, sometimes they do. I remember a manufacturing firm in New England that was going to have to shut down operations for several months because of a fire that had swept through their plant. The business owner chose to keep paying his employees even while they were closed, and that, quite rightly, made news. But for the most part, companies that do business in a sound, ethical fashion just continue to do so, and nobody writes stories about them. We hear about the big ethical problems like Enron. And when the safety issues came up about Ford Explorers, the news reports portrayed Ford Motor Company and Firestone as more worried about placing blame on one another than they were about solving the problem. Whether it was true or not, that's how it was reported. Now the funny thing to me is, as those same companies have taken greater and greater steps to ensure the safety of the people who buy their vehicles, we haven't heard much about that in the news.

Sometimes corporate America and organizational America get bad raps simply because we focus too much on the negative stories. Of course, the negative and the sensational sell papers, get people to watch the news, and to listen to radio talk shows. Just the same, if we're trying to become more successful on a personal basis, our focus needs to be on wanting to do things right and to do the right things. Don't let what gets reported determine what you should do.

Wright

In some of your materials, you talk about personal and emotional debt, about starting over, about doing the right thing, about getting there the hard way. What do you mean by "emotional debt"?

Lust

Emotional debt is what you owe yourself. When you cheat yourself by not doing your best, by giving an incomplete effort, or by taking shortcuts, I believe you create a debt against the person you could be. If you continue to build that debt without paying yourself back through some extended, conscious, and gratifying effort to be better, you can be just as bankrupt as the person who spends more money than he or she earns. The unfortunate truth is, we don't have a Chapter 7 legal bankruptcy filing available to absolve us from what we owe to ourselves. We can't wash that plate clean with a simple court order. The only way to clear the emotional debt we owe ourselves is with an effort to do our best that at least equals all the times we have fallen short.

Wright

How much attention do you give to the concept of forgiveness when you teach emotional debt?

Lust

Forgiveness is a big key. What we have to consider, however, is whether we seek forgiveness because we desire to move forward and improve, or merely to get something unpleasant out of the way.

Earlier, I mentioned Chapter 7 legal filings in a passing comment. But that's a good example of what I mean. If you are somebody who is bankrupt financially, you have spent more money than you can repay. Today, it's almost too convenient to fill out a few legal papers and somehow be absolved of that debt. They actually use the term forgiveness: "We'll forgive the debt." But if you don't learn your lesson and change your behavior, you'll make the same bad decisions again and soon be in the same position.

This is what lenders fear, especially today. With my banking background I can speak to this. If someone has felt comfortable about filing bankruptcy once, what's to stop that person from doing it a second time? As a lender charged with safeguarding the assets of an institution's investors, it is a heavy burden to have to determine whether someone who has not demonstrated good financial habits in the past somehow now has changed. In this case, the lender says, "If they've not paid their bills in the past, why should I lend them money in the future?" The only responsible way to say "Yes" to forgiveness is if the formerly bankrupt borrower has demonstrated a conscious effort to replace bad habits. Make sure that if you are seeking forgiveness for an emotional debt, it is because you have made the same effort to change and not just because you simply want to forget past transgressions.

Wright

You and I have similar backgrounds in that we have both been in banking. I remember one of the most difficult things for me to understand was that I used to make loans to people to consolidate debts and sometimes cut their payments from thousands down to hundreds of dollars a month. All of a sudden, six months to a year later, they would be in the same situation again because their behavior had not changed.

Lust

That's right. I can understand that. In fact, that is the basis from which my *Financial Fitness* program sprang. I was that person. Coming out of school, I had a lot of debts and some bad spending habits. I did what you just described. I knew from my work at the bank that it wasn't wise to carry credit card balances at high interest rates, so I would take out a bank loan to consolidate my debts.

After doing that, a person doesn't make a conscious choice to say, "Okay, now I'm going to go out and run up the balance on my credit cards again." But pretty soon, you think the car needs some work and you open that bottle with the genie again and the credit card has a little balance on it. Then you think, "I'll just put this dinner on my card because I'll be able to pay that off next month." Then it's a gift for that special someone, or yourself, that you justify because "it just can't wait." Then you might find a sale you just can't pass up. And pretty soon you are right back in the same boat. What needs to happen is a fundamental shift in your priorities and your decision making.

Altman

There are always places to spend credit cards and money— especially if you're a lady!

Kevin, there have been more workshops, audio and video programs, and articles written about customer service than any other topic in the past ten years, yet customer service seems to be at an all-time low. Do you agree with that statement? And if so, why is it so bad?

Lust

Well, I agree to the extent that there are plenty of bad examples out there. But once again, I like to seek out the good examples. One reason why customer service that's not good continues to exist is because we, as customers, accept it. Partially, as a consumer, it's our choice. I think what we often do is choose convenience over service. If we've got a dry cleaner that is not providing us good service, but we continue to go there because it's on our way home, then I think we're responsible for continuing to receive bad service. I'm a big believer in the power of the marketplace, and if we took a stand against bad service and said, "We're not going to shop here anymore," one of two things is going to happen: either the places that are providing poor service are going to change, or they are going to go out of business.

Wright

Kevin, in most of your presentations you teach principles and methods of budgeting, communications, and integrity. It seems to me that these are relationship issues as well. Do you help families stay together by being more responsible as a happenstance of your work, or is it intentional on your part?

Lust

I think that is a great question. It really did start off as happenstance. By that I mean I didn't intend consciously to say,

"Okay, here's the relationship piece." But the more I study successful people and organizations as I develop my material, the more I realize that balance I spoke about earlier is an essential ingredient.

You'll remember that our relationships play an important role in CPR. Let's take financial fitness as an example. With regard to financial fitness in relationships, one of the single largest problems mentioned in divorce cases is conflict about money. One party has one philosophy about money, the other party has a different philosophy, and they just can't agree. If the couple can find ways to be jointly more disciplined financially, to make better use of their money and investments, and to communicate more about money, spending, and investing, that problem goes away. Through teaching about financial fitness, we make a positive relationship contribution.

In fact, any of the other topics that I address—communication, negotiation, life balance, or even management—can be interpreted to find within them ways to support family relationships and personal relationships. I think the more we learn about those subjects at work, the better chance we have to be successful at home, if only we'd bring them home with us. That's the problem. A lot of people learn those good lessons and they practice those good skills at work, but they never apply them anywhere else.

Wright

One of the problems I've noticed throughout my life is that financial problems reach out to every area of our lives. It's hard to be romantic when you're thinking about not making your house payment tomorrow. It's hard to have a good conversation with your wife if you're going to talk about money, especially if your bills are past due.

Lust

It sort of hangs over your head, and you just feel perpetually anxious. I know how I feel when I have a bill that's due and I don't have the money for it. It's a sense of anxiously waiting rather than eagerly waiting. There's a big difference between the two words "anxious" and "eager." Anxiety is the nervous anticipation of what we do not want to happen. It is what causes personal stress. Eagerness is the joyful hope for that which we most desire. We see too many cases where money problems have brought the anxiety that causes people to make very poor decisions.

Altman

It does create so much personal tension between couples. You have such a great topic. Dave Ramsey is definitely doing well with this topic at present, isn't he?

Lust

Yes, I've heard a lot of his work.

Altman

Kevin, with our *Mission Possible!* talk show and book, we are trying to encourage people in our audience to be better, live better, and be more fulfilled by listening to the examples of our guests. Is there anyone in your life who has made a difference for you and helped you to be a better person?

Lust

There are dozens of people. Unfortunately, I can't introduce all the members of our audience to every one of them. I wish that I could. Of all that collected wisdom, though, there have been some great lessons that I learned first from my parents. That's the place where I'd start. I'd like everybody out there to have a chance to say hello to them, although they live in a very small town in north central Illinois, and they'd probably wonder why everybody was streaming by their driveway all of a sudden.

Altman

What are your parents' names?

Lust

My dad's name is Al, and my mom's name is Ann.

Wright

Well, we'll say good morning to them.

Altman

Hello, Al and Ann.

Wright

We took care of that, didn't we?

Lust

Well, that's good. People always say, "Hi, Mom" on TV, but I like to say, "Hi, Mom and Dad."

If there are any good things that have happened as a result of the terrorist attacks on the World Trade Center and on the Pentagon, one of the things that I've seen as a positive is that we have started to recognize what I have heard referred to as "citizen heroes." We're taking a fresh look at firefighters, police officers, EMT workers, and even moms and dads. These are the people around us who, often at great sacrifice to themselves, take such great care of us. They all legitimately can be referred to as heroes. I would encourage people to look around in their own lives for the people who could be a positive influence on them.

We used to talk about sports figures as heroes. I'm surrounded here in my office by some of my personal public figure heroes. I've got statues of Winston Churchill, Mark Twain, Thomas Jefferson, and Dwight Eisenhower. But there are also pictures of my dad's parents who came from Sweden, and of my mom's parents who came from a little place called Slovenia, which was a part of Yugoslavia.

My mom's mother, the little, old, sweet, gentle "Gramma" of my memory, left her village in the mountains for the first time at age sixteen to get onto the first boat she had ever seen and sail across an ocean. She then found her way halfway across a continent, on her own, to meet a sister whom she hadn't seen for three years and wasn't sure was still there or even alive. For what reason, I don't even know. I never asked her why she came. But I suspect it's because she thought things were better here and that she could build a better life for herself and for her family.

This is a heroic act. I wonder how I can make that same sort of progress toward "that something better." What can I do so that one day my son or perhaps his children can feel the same way about me as I feel about my grandmother?

Altman

That is definitely a leap of faith.

Lust

It certainly is . . . it's a leap made into an unknown. I suspect that's just what a lot of immigrants did, my grandmother included. The thing that I find most amazing about my parents' and grandparents' generations is that they accomplished such great things without much fanfare. They seldom felt the need to trumpet their achievements or to complain about their hardships. They just did what they had to do and moved on.

We've heard a great deal about "the greatest generation" in recent months, and rightly so. The same comment has been made again and again by the soldiers and sailors who suffered horribly in battle, by the wives and parents who waited anxiously at home for word from overseas, by the factory workers who turned out the arms while suffering through rationing and shortages: "It's just what we were supposed to do." They didn't look at it as some big sacrifice. It was just what came next.

I think sometimes we get a little wrapped up in ourselves today. We view every minor thing we do as some earth-shattering, monumental sacrifice, when, in fact, it's just what comes next. I think if more people would approach the decisions they make in their life with a "Well, what's next?" attitude, we'd all be a lot better off.

Wright

I would never suggest that anyone ever bomb anything, anytime, anywhere; yet at the expense of sounding like I might want to, do you think that 9-11 ultimately will be good for our country?

Lust

I think that it already has been. First, of course, it is tragic and horrible and awful and despicable. The losses that we, as a country, have felt are horrible, especially for those individuals who lost family members in the bombings. The vivid images I have of all those people holding their little photos behind the television reporters will stay with me forever. The good that's come of it is that we really have adopted a sense of mission.

I co-authored a book called *Motivational Leaders,* and my chapter was all about mission. In it, I describe how a strong mission can become our most valuable decision maker. Once we decide what is most important to us, then future decisions automatically become easier.

We've seen that to a degree in our country. With our newfound sense of national mission, I would hope that we would be better able to make sound decisions about our national priorities. From a military perspective, certainly, we've kept the mission focus on a daily basis and made our decisions accordingly. This concrete sense of mission can aid in anyone's decision making. Decide in your own life what is most important to you, and then make day-to-day, minute-by-minute decisions, always with an eye on what ultimately is your major destination.

Wright

That's one reason, if not the main reason, that Alex and I do this talk show and book. We've talked to some great people, even celebrities, who are just devastated by the effects of 9-11. But they all, speaking in unison, say there is so much good that has come out of it already, and people in the United States are looking at, as you called them, heroes in other fields rather than people like Michael Jordan. There's nothing wrong with Michael Jordan; I love to watch him play basketball. But when you think about the firemen . . . you knew theirs was a dangerous job, but you didn't really realize how dangerous until the news coverage started after 9-11.

Lust

Isn't it great to return to the day when we look at a police officer and say, "He's our friend"? We had gotten away from that because all we heard were negative stories about incompetence or corruption. While these cases have always been the exception, they were the ones being reported. Now we're hearing again of the very, very good things police officers do.

I'll share this example with you. My sister-in-law had been planning her son's Cub Scouts Blue and Gold Banquet. We were talking about potential themes, and in just a few minutes we arrived at "Citizen Heroes." She's going to bring in some ex-Cub Scouts who now have careers in firefighting, law enforcement, and emergency medical services and ask them to share what they learned when they were Scouts that still helps them today. We never even would have considered this as a theme prior to September of last year. It never would have occurred to us. Now, I think it is going to be the best banquet they've ever had.

Wright

In a follow-up to Alex's last question, what do you think makes a great mentor? In other words, are there characteristics that mentors seem to have in common?

Lust

In my experience with the mentors I've enjoyed being around, I've found that the good ones listen as much as they talk. Sometimes people confuse mentoring with someone telling you how you do things. Particularly within formal mentor programs, you'll find a person who is assigned a mentor or assigned to be a mentor who misunderstands the process. They think that the mentor's job is to tell the person they are mentoring how everything should be done, how to avoid every problem and pitfall, and "this is the way we've always done it." That's not the case at all.

Good mentors are people who take the time to understand the challenges the persons they are mentoring are facing. They take the time to listen for their associates' frustrations and to celebrate their successes. They take the time to care for them so they can bring forth their good qualities and skills and help them use them the best that they can. It's not just an instructional role; it's very much a relationship role.

Wright

We were talking to Brian Tracy recently, and he told us, as you just did, that there is a lot of difference between a mentor and a consultant.

Lust

That's right. You know, you were talking about personal heroes, and I would certainly classify Brian Tracy as one of those. Following his goal-setting exercises is how I got into the speaking business. I can remember sitting in my basement office in the little house the bank and I owned back in 1989, writing out exactly what I wanted to do. Lo and behold, here I am, years later, still doing it.

Altman

When you consider the choices you have made down through the years, has faith played an important role in your life?

Lust

It has. I believe that my faith and my family provide the grounding that gives me the strength to make choices and take chances that might involve a little bit of risk. I have always known that even if I falter in something, my mom and dad are still there, my brothers and my wife's family are still there. They are very, very close to us and, in fact, many of them live in the city where we live. Those people are still going to be around no matter what. They like it when they see my picture on the cover of a book. They enjoy it when they hear me on the radio or see me on television. But that's not what we talk about. It is just as important to them that I'm around, whether I'm doing those things or not. This kind of support and grounding is what gives me the desire and confidence to keep stretching.

Altman

There's nothing like that love and support behind you, no matter what.

Lust

That's right, and those are the lessons that are taught us in our faith.

Wright

Most people in our culture are fascinated with the new TV shows about being a survivor. What has been the greatest comeback you have made from adversity in your career . . . or your life, for that matter?

Lust

It's actually in both. When I left my banking career, it was through an unusual set of circumstances. There is no getting around the fact that I was fired from my last job as personnel director for the bank holding company where I was working, but it was the strangest firing I've ever seen. My boss and I agreed that the job that I had been promoted to at the bank had turned out not to be the best position for me. It was a very detail-oriented role, and I was more of a big picture person. My boss needed somebody to pay attention to the day-to-day, individual issues, and I was much more interested in thinking about and creating a better future for the whole place. But even though he decided that I should leave, he didn't want me to go right away. I remember soon after we had made the decision, somebody asked, "You didn't get fired, did you?" and I had to say, "Well, when my boss says to me, 'We're going to have to terminate your employment,' I take that as I'm fired."

What made this all unique in my mind was that as we sat in that room on a particular day and my boss said that this wasn't working out for us and that I needed to go, he also said that he wanted me to stick around. So for six and a half weeks after I was fired, I was still on board, working hard, doing the right things, and, mercifully, getting paid. Obviously, it was devastating, nonetheless. Anytime you hear you didn't do a good job, it's no fun. That is what they were telling me, even though at the same time my boss was telling me all the good things I had done as well. But when you hear the bad part, it's devastating.

This particularly felt true for me. I've been an achiever since my early school days and had good success at nearly everything I tried, especially those things that I enjoyed. I really enjoyed my job at the bank, and I enjoyed the people that I worked with. To hear that I hadn't been successful was a huge setback for me. I shed more than a few tears and felt angry and betrayed and more than a little alone over the days immediately after I heard that.

But that didn't last long. It was a remarkable coincidence that my boss made the decision that he made, at the time that he made it. At that same point, I already was thinking of moving on. I mentioned Brian Tracy earlier in our discussion. In February of 1989, I completed the goal-setting exercises Tracy assigns in his "Psychology of Achievement" program. From that, I made a decision that I wanted to work as a trainer and move to Chicago. I had spent some time up there in April, not-so-coincidentally right around opening day of the baseball season. (To give you a sense of why I wanted to move to Chicago, I love the Cubs.) That spring I spent time in the city with some of my buddies who were living there. I said, "You know, I really could live here."

I took the rest of my vacation at the end of the baseball season and spent another two weeks interviewing for work in Chicago. It was the day after I came back from that trip that my boss told me I would be leaving the bank. He didn't know that I was already thinking about that. So I was already moving forward, and I accepted my new position as a speaker and consultant for an international training corporation on the very afternoon that we held my going-away party at the bank.

That was the unique and special thing about this entire ordeal. When they said it was time to go, that ended up being the final push that I needed. I had thought about going, and I wanted to go, but prior to getting fired I merely was planning to move to Chicago; I hadn't committed to it. Then, when I had my decision made for me, I truly could move forward. I looked at it all as a sign that this was the right move. And it has been, unequivocally. That move turned out to be the foundation for each of the wonderful things that have happened since then in my life. From that negative experience I've learned that in any situation, if you look hard enough, there are going to be some seeds that can help you gain benefits equal to, if not far surpassing, the loss you may have felt. It took me a long time even to be able to confess to people that I got fired from a job, let alone put it in print, but it has turned into the single best opportunity in my life.

Wright

A lot of people who move to Chicago think it is a religious calling to witness the gods of the Bulls and the Cubbies.

Lust

There is a lot of praying going on, I'll tell you that.

Altman

If you could have a platform and tell our audience something you believe would help or encourage them, what would you say?

Lust

I'd go back to my first comment. I'd tell people to pay attention to all areas of their lives. If you're trying to be successful in your career, if you're working hard, paying attention to where you're headed and reaching your goals, that's great. At the same time, you're going to feel pretty hollow if you get there and find that you've neglected to take care of your relationships or to build the strong foundation of family and friends that can help you enjoy those successes. And certainly, if you've not paid attention to yourself, to your personal development, your health, wellness, and sanity, you're not going to be able to enjoy your successes in any other area.

So pay attention to all areas of your life and don't try to fool yourself along the way. You know whether you are doing the work or not. That's integrity—doing your best when no one is looking. At the end of the day, when you tally up what you've done or not done, no matter if anyone else sees your results, you have to read them yourself. Don't try to fool yourself. You either did the work or didn't do the work. In all areas of your life, your career, your personal life, and your relationships, you'll know if you did what you had to, and you'll enjoy the results if you have. Make the effort to get the results. And then remember just one more thing: Above all else, life should be fun. Enjoy yourself along the way.

Wright

This has been a fast half hour, Kevin. Alex and I really appreciate your being with us today.

We've been talking to Kevin Lust, who is a professional trainer and inspirational speaker, and a very successful one at that. We have found out today just why he is.

Kevin, thank you so much for being on our program.

Altman

Yes, Kevin, and we expect to see big things from you in the future. You are a delightful person.

Lust

Keep looking; I'll be there.

Kevin Lust
Lust Development Group
Suite 349, 2745 South Sixth Street
Springfield, Illinois 62703-4071 USA
Telephone: 888.241.5878
Fax: 217.241.5879
kevinlust@kevinlust.com
www.kevinlust.com

Chapter 6

Dr. Barry Sears

Best-selling author of The Zone,
*Dr. Barry Sears is president of
The Sears Technology Group, which
spearheads research into drug delivery
systems and other related topics. He has
begun work on more books and is
developing an educational Zone
program for his Web site.*

The Interview

David E. Wright (Wright)

Today we are talking with Dr. Barry Sears, a leading authority
in the field of drug delivery and dietary control of hormonal
response. A former research scientist at the Boston University
School of Medicine and the Massachusetts Institute of Technology,
Dr. Sears has dedicated the past twenty-five years of his research
efforts to the development of innovative drug delivery technologies
using lipids. His landmark book, *The Zone,* sold more than one and
a half million in hardcover and became the number one bestseller
on the *New York Times* list. He also authored *Mastering the Zone,*

which also became a *New York Times* bestseller, and *Zone Perfect Meals in Minutes*. To date, more than three million hardcover copies of *Zone* books have been sold in the United States. Dr. Barry Sears, welcome to *Mission Possible!*.

Dr. Barry Sears (Sears)
Thank you very much.

Alexandria Altman (Altman)
Welcome, Dr. Sears.

Sears
Thank you.

Wright
Dr. Sears, just what are lipids, and how do they affect us?

Sears
Lipids are really fats, and for the last twenty years, Americans have been told that fats are villains, and to avoid them at all cost in their diets. Unfortunately, we never realized how important these lipids are, because they control every aspect of our lives, whether it is our brains, our hearts, our immune systems, or even our emotions. Therefore, if we really want to eventually take control of ourselves, we have to basically make sure we are eating the right type of fat on a daily basis.

Altman
Can you tell us what you think the right fats are?

Sears
Actually, your great-grandmother told you two generations ago when she told your parents that they had to take their tablespoon

of cod liver oil every day. It's the most disgusting food known to man, but it contains certain fats. These are called longchain omega-3 fats, which are the keys to maintaining health and longevity as we age.

Altman

You've said that foods are drugs. Can you explain what you mean by that?

Sears

In many ways that's being derogatory to food, because food affects hormones, and hormones are a hundred times more powerful than any drug known to medical science. So that makes food the most powerful drug you'll ever come into contact with. Unfortunately, the door can swing both ways. Food is the most powerful drug you'll every come into contact with to enhance your life; but conversely, if you make the wrong food choices and generate the wrong hormonal responses, it could be your worst nightmare. The rules that govern how food controls hormones cannot change and will not change in our lifetime.

Wright

I remember reading in one of your books an interesting segment where you were talking about the Egyptians who changed their eating habits and got five inches shorter. I wish I remembered more about it. Can you explain what you were talking about?

Sears

Genetically, we are really no different than our ancestors were a hundred thousand years ago. Only in the last ten thousand years were grains actually introduced in the diet. Now we have a very clear understanding of what happened when that occurrence took place, and the answer contains a lot of negative things. The first thing that happened was mankind shrunk. The average height of Neo-Paleolithic man about ten thousand years ago was about six feet. The average height of Neo-Paleolithic woman was about five feet six inches. Once grains were introduced, we saw shrinkage across the board on humanity.

The second thing that happened was that many of the so-called diseases of modern civilization, like heart disease, made their first appearance with the advent of grain. That's why when we look at Egyptian mummies that have visceral remains, we find widespread evidence of arterial lesions, even though the average life span of an Egyptian was only twenty years.

The mummies also tell us that the Egyptians were actually fat. How can we tell? They have extra rolls of skin around their midsection. We can estimate that the amount of obesity in ancient Egypt was not all that different from what we see in modern-day America. The irony of that statement is that the Egyptian diet is virtually the identical diet that is being recommended to every American citizen by the government—a diet rich in grain, some fruits and vegetables, small amounts of protein, and avoidance of fats at all costs. What we are doing is simply repeating history. If the Egyptians were brought up on that diet, then according to the government's dietary recommendations they should have been the healthiest people on the face of the earth; however, anthropology and archeological records show otherwise.

Wright

I remember reading that Egyptians had a life span of twenty years. I almost dropped the book.

Sears

Again, it was only recently—about the turn of the last century—that the average life span in America was forty-six or forty-seven years. We have dramatically increased our life span primarily by decreasing childhood mortality and mortality of women during childbirth. We haven't done a real good job of working on the upper end, which is the quality of life as we age. That's the real goal of twenty-first century medicine, to make sure we have a full and healthy life as long as possible. How do we do that? We go back to our drug of choice for the future, and that drug will be food.

Wright

Dr. Sears, you've sold over three million books having to do with diet and weight control. What are the major reasons Americans are so overweight?

Sears

I think the reasons are contained in a number of factors. First and foremost, we don't have time anymore. One of the primary goals was to have our entire social structure built around the foods we eat. That basically has been sent to the back forty, because no one has time to gather together and, more importantly, allow time to make correctly-balanced meals.

Second, we are told by our government, "Take fat out of your diet." We Americans are very proactive; we have taken fat out of our diets. We are eating less fat now than at any time in our history. Unfortunately, we have replaced that fat with fat-free carbohydrates that increase the hormone insulin, and that is the reason we become fat. Fat doesn't make us fat. What makes us fat and keeps us fat is excessive production of the hormone insulin. The more carbohydrates we eat, the more insulin we make. If we use some common sense, we'd realize this. How do we fatten cattle? We feed them lots and lots of low-fat grain. How do we fatten humans? We feed them lots and lots of low-fat grain in the form of bagels and pasta.

Altman

Can you give our audience a basic rundown of breakfast, lunch, and dinner—what you consider a hormonally correct balanced diet?

Sears

Let me give you a typical day in the Zone for the average female. She might start the day off with a six-egg light omelet. She'll throw away the yolks and replace those yolks with two teaspoons of olive oil. She'll have two-thirds cup of oatmeal and a cup of strawberries. That's a fairly hefty breakfast. For lunch she'll have a chicken Caesar salad with three ounces of chicken breast, but she'll need to add about two cups of steamed vegetables and a piece of fruit for dessert. At five o'clock, she'll have a small hormonal snack of two hard-boiled eggs, in which she'll take out the yolk and replace that yolk with hummus, which is chickpeas plus olive oil. For dinner she might have five ounces of steamed salmon, four cups of steamed vegetables, and a cup of fruit for dessert, and before she goes to bed, a glass of wine and a small piece of cheese.

Wright

That's a lot of food.

Sears

That is a lot of food. Now if you calculate the calories, it's about 1200 calories per day.

Altman

If we start eating like that daily, do our bodies and hormonal systems quickly adapt to this diet?

Sears

It definitely does, and we now know how rapidly it does, because Harvard Medical School has told us. The answer is one meal.

Altman

One meal to change your life . . . is that what you are saying?

Sears

Yes, one meal. Hormonally, you are only as good as your last meal, and hormonally you are only as good as your next meal. It's like taking a drug. Drugs only work when you take them at the right dosage and at the right time. For example, if you are taking high blood pressure medication, would you take it all on Saturday afternoon? Probably not. Your doctor says, "I want you to take it three times a day to maintain a Zone of the drug in the bloodstream." That's what you're looking at doing with food. Every time you eat, you want to get the right balance of protein and carbohydrates to get the most hormonal cluck for the buck.

Now, how do you do that? All you need is one hand and one eye, and here are all the rules your listeners ever need to know. At each meal you divide your plate into three sections. On one-third of the plate, you put some low-fat protein that is no bigger and no thicker than the palm of your hand. On the other two-thirds of the plate, you fill it till it is overflowing with fruits and vegetables, and you add a dash—which is a small amount—of heart-healthy mono-unsaturated fat, which could be olive oil, slivered almonds, or even guacamole. And there you have it—a drug that will keep the hormone insulin in that Zone for the next four to six hours so you aren't hungry and you have peak mental acuity.

Wright

I thought if I ate less I'd lose weight.

Sears

You can always lose weight. You can cut off your left arm and you would lose weight. But if you really want to lose excess body fat, the only way to do that is to lower insulin, and the only way you can lower insulin is to balance your plate every time you eat.

Wright

One of your books I have not read is *Zone-Perfect Meals in Minutes*. Is it a cookbook, and is it in bookstores today?

Sears

Yes, it is. As a matter-of-fact, it's not so much a cookbook, but a book I wrote for my diabetic patients. What it has is a hundred and fifty "drugs," known as recipes, each one saying, "Eat this recipe and don't think." In our diabetic patients, with whom we use it as an educational manual, what are some of the results? In about six to eight weeks, we see every blood parameter associated with diabetes begin to normalize.

We have two epidemics taking place in our society today. One is called obesity and the other is Type 2 diabetes. Both of them can be corrected almost overnight simply if we're willing to treat food with the same respect we treat any prescription drug. It doesn't mean that it has to taste like a drug; we are paying attention to simply balancing the plate the best we can, using the food we like to eat at every meal.

Altman

So we need to think insulin and not fat, right?

Sears

Exactly. Think of two words your grandmother taught you, *balance* and *moderation*. Look at your plate every time you eat, and put a moderate amount of calories on that plate. The easiest way to put a moderate amount of calories on a plate is basically to eat lots of fruits and vegetables and go easy on the grains, starches, bread, and bagels.

Let me give you another example. Anyone can eat one cup of pasta, but eating twelve cups of steamed broccoli is hard work. They both contain the same amount of carbohydrates, but which of those two carbohydrates are you more likely to overconsume? Pasta. So by having lots of fruits and vegetables, you have a built-in mechanism that gives you a great volume of food but not too much carbohydrates, and the less carbohydrates you eat, the less insulin you make.

Altman

Dr. Sears, you have worked with lots of athletes. Is it true that athletes perform better on a high-carb, low-fat diet?

Sears

Actually, athletes perform better on a moderate carbohydrate diet. We always try to swing to the extreme and talk about high carbohydrates or high protein, yet we know through common sense that neither one of those makes sense. What does make sense is to get something between the extremes, which is usually a moderate carbohydrate program. When we work with world-class athletes—and the ones I have personally worked with have won twenty-one gold medals in the last three Olympics—we moderate their diet. Really, their diet is not very different from that of a Type 2 diabetic patient, except athletes eat larger amounts of protein because they have more muscle mass. They eat larger amounts of carbohydrates because they need more due to the level of activity, but the balance of protein and carbohydrates remains exactly the same.

Wright

I don't want that statement to go unnoticed by our listeners and readers. As I was reading about you, I learned that you had worked for years with the Stanford swimming team. Also, I heard that you were in no small part responsible for twenty-one gold medals. That's quite impressive.

Sears

Again, it was a very fortunate circumstance. We had the ability to work with world-class athletes and to figure out what real people will eat. (After all, if you can't get a world-class athlete to make dietary adjustments, how can you expect the average person on the street to do the same thing?) By working with world-class athletes, we found some of the different motivational techniques that can get people to say that magical phrase, "I can do this." Once a person can do it, he or she can do it on a lifetime basis. It's kind of like riding a bicycle. At first it seems so difficult, but once you learn to balance that bicycle, you never forget.

Altman

Dr. Sears, high-protein diets are popular. Are they effective?

Sears

Millions of people in our country over the last thirty years have lost weight on high-protein diets. Unfortunately, the same millions of people have gained that weight back, if not more. They all can't be weak-willed ninnies, so something else is going on here.

When you are on a high-protein diet, which has virtually no carbohydrates, you generate an abnormal state in the body called ketosis, and you lose a lot of water. The longer you stay in this ketosis format, you turn your fat cells into fat magnets. It doesn't happen the first day or the first week or the first month, but usually about three months out, your fat cells begin adapting to become fat magnets. You see weight loss very steady for the first three months, then it levels off, even though you're still eating the high-protein, low-carbohydrate diet; then weight begins to increase. The reason is that you have made biochemical adaptations that virtually force the body to begin accumulating body fat. So we know high-protein diets don't work.

So what's left? Basically, what's in between. That's what we call the Zone—not too high and not too low.

Wright

Dr. Sears, with our *Mission Possible!* talk show and book, we are trying to encourage people in our audience to be better, live better, and be more fulfilled by listening to the examples of our guests. Is there anything or anyone in your life who has made a difference for you and helped you to be a better person?

Sears

I think as you go through life—assuming you like the way your life has turned out—you can always look and find a number of people who have made significant contributions. Obviously, my family is number one. The people you look back to are your teachers, the people who basically tried to parlay their insights; and if you were intelligent enough to listen, you would have incorporated those insights into your daily activities. Looking back at many of my teachers, ranging from grammar school to graduate school, I can see there were individuals who pointed me in the right direction. You can ask a lot of questions about how things happened, but why things happened is more important. Those are the lessons you look to, and you thank the people who basically pointed you in that direction.

Wright

I'm always interested in the answer to that question. We've had a lot of people say they've read biographies of great people, most of whom are dead now, and use them as their examples. But we had one lady who hit it squarely. She said it was just a matter of being interested in someone. She mentioned teachers who took an interest in her. Not only were they good examples and role models for her, but they also took an interest in her.

Sears

I look at the work I've done. I consider myself a very good scientist, but I consider myself an excellent teacher. An excellent teacher has to like people and have an interest in helping them help themselves. I've been very fortunate that the subject I write about has allowed me to teach to a much larger number of people that they can take control of their lives if they choose to. The teachers who influenced me made me what I am today—a teacher.

Altman

Dr. Sears, I have one other question about the Zone Diet. Does it work for basically every body type? There seems to be a new phase of diet plans that say if you're this body type, eat this; or if you're that body type, eat that—kind of like the ABCs of body types. Does the Zone Diet work for every body type?

Sears

The answer to that is yes. People tend to overcomplicate. What's going on inside our bodies is very complex, but how to orchestrate it is very simple. Other than basically the amount of protein you eat and, therefore, the amount of carbohydrates, the Zone is universal for the small child, the elderly, the world-class athlete, the Type 2 diabetic. What we're looking to achieve is a center of universality, and that's saying that once we control our hormones by the food we eat, we control our lives. Therefore, whether they say, "You're body type A, and you're body type K," we need to think, "Wait a minute; we're all human beings, and we're all controlled by these hormones. All we have to do is learn to balance our food every time we eat. By doing so, we control our hormones and control our future."

Altman

Sounds like we all need to be in the Zone.

Sears

We all do, because this is what made us human in the first place. It's less complicated to do than people think; it's just a matter of responsibility. In the Zone, we're not as much treating chronic disease as moving ourselves toward a state of wellness, and that's where twenty-first century medicine is going, I believe. We quantify chronic disease. We have thousands of drugs to treat chronic disease, but we had no way, until recently, to really define what wellness is. I think blood tests will dictate the Zone. The Zone is not some mythical place in our bodies. Blood tests will tell us, and those same blood tests will also become the medical definition to wellness. If so, we can change our medical practice to promoting wellness as opposed to treating disease.

Altman

Dr. Sears, what do you think makes up a great mentor? In other words, are there characteristics that mentors seem to have in common?

Sears

I think there are. I would say the characteristics are (1) they care about others, and (2) they take great care in imparting lessons they've learned to others. Often times there are great mentors but very poor students. You can lead many horses to water, but not necessarily all of them will drink. I think that there are many great mentors out there, but there are few students who are willing to take the time to listen to their wisdom.

Wright

Dr. Sears, this is off the subject a little bit. I talked to someone in your office who told me that your next book, *The Omega Rx Zone,* will be coming out in 2002. Could you tell us a little about it? How does it differ from your other books?

Sears

It is really the work I've been doing the last three years, using a brand-new type of fish oil that's not yet available on the market but has been available for research purposes, which I call "pharmaceutical-grade." We ask, How far can we take this fish oil? What can it do to the behavior and, more importantly, the treatment of neurological diseases?

What is our greatest fear as we age? It is the brain giving out before the body does. We've been able to stabilize insulin by balancing the plate at each meal and adding high-dose, pharmaceutical-grade fish oil, and we've seen dramatic changes in a wide number of neurological conditions: dementia, attention deficit disorder, depression, Parkinson's, multiple sclerosis. Other investigators using the same type of oil have reported similar changes.

It goes back to something as simple as this: Can taking fish oil every day have a great impact on our future as human beings? The answer turns out to be a resounding "Yes!" But you have to have a high-quality material, because—depending on the disease condition—it may require significant levels. For example, one of the biggest problems we have with children today is attention deficit disorder. We have millions of kids going to school each day using Ritalin to try to control their behavior. Yet the children we worked with in no more than four weeks were able to reverse their behavior simply by changing their diet and taking high doses of fish oil. Now, what is "high-dose"? It is close to six tablespoons of cod liver oil. But nobody in their right mind would ever take any cod liver oil. Now we have high-dose fish oil that has virtually no taste, no flavor, so it is much easier to take.

Wright

My mother died of Alzheimer's; my mother-in-law has it now. Would that include Alzheimer's?

Sears

Definitely. We had the opportunity of working with a nursing home. In most nursing homes, the people who are sent there usually have a certain amount, if not a great amount, of Alzheimer's already present. In every case we've seen reversals. Why this is important is that a cloud comes between you and your parents so that they no longer recognize you. You think, "I only wish I had the time to talk to them about things. I only wish they could listen to what I have to say." But what you begin to see, in a fairly short period of time is that cloud lifting and a return to the world of living.

Wright

It's not only the dementia of the one who has Alzheimer's, but the effect on the caregivers and the family as well. It's one thing to say that your mother *can't* recognize you, but it's another thing when she actually *doesn't* recognize you. That really does hurt.

Sears

Yes, it does. That's why the most satisfying thing is seeing families basically connect. What you are doing with a high-dose fish oil is taking detours around the areas and finding new neural connections. Why is this important? Because the fish oil contains certain fats that the brain must have. Without an adequate amount of those fats, the brain cannot make new connections.

Wright

When you say "high-dose," are you referring to quality of the fish oil or quantity?

Sears

Both. Most fish oils available in health food stores you would never take very much of because there are simply too many impurities. Only with the advent of what I call pharmaceutical-grade fish oil can you go to higher dosages, because the purity is that much greater. Then things really and truly begin to happen.

Altman

Most people are fascinated with the new TV shows about being a survivor. What has been the greatest comeback you have made from adversity in your career or life?

Sears

I guess I would say it was about twenty years ago. I got this bee in my bonnet that food could be a very powerful drug. At the time, I thought I was a pretty well-recognized scientist at MIT, developing an international reputation in drug delivery systems. So I started spending more time investigating that idea and quickly became shunned as a charlatan. For about fifteen years, I wandered in the wilderness asking myself, "Why am I doing all this?" But at the same time, I knew the payoff would be great if I could just find that Rosetta Stone of protein-carbohydrate that could unlock our future.

Again, being a survivor means having enough perseverance, enough belief in yourself to hang on in spite of great odds. The German philosopher Schopenhauer said, probably a hundred and fifty years ago, "All truth passes through three stages. First, it is ridiculed. Second, it is violently opposed. Third, it is accepted as being self-evident." The idea to balance our plate and control insulin—I was ridiculed for many years when I wrote my first book, *The Zone*—caused a firestorm of controversy. Now, some six years after the book was first published, it's accepted as truth.

Likewise, the need for high-dose fish oil will generate the same amount of controversy. But the research being done by myself and other scientists throughout the world is pointing clearly that this becomes our truth for the future. By doing something as simple as balancing our plate and taking our high-dose fish oil, we can reach our full human potential. That means not only being more well, but, more importantly, having far greater emotional control and stability, which is really the essence of what makes humans. We care about others. There's a very thin veneer between being human and being an animal. That veneer is controlled by certain morality hormones in our brains, which can be increased by the intake of fish oil.

Wright

I could ask you questions all day long, Dr. Sears, but we've come to the end of our program. We are going to have to do this again some time.

Sears

I look forward to that; hopefully we can speak again. I think the concepts we've touched upon affect a wide spectrum of our society.

Wright

Today we have been talking to Dr. Barry Sears, a leading authority in the field of drug delivery and dietary control of hormonal response. We certainly do appreciate your appearance on *Mission Possible!* today, Dr. Sears. Thank you so much for coming

Sears

Thank you for the opportunity.

Altman

Dr. Sears, you are very inspirational. Next time I talk to you, I will be in the Zone.

Sears

Excellent!

Dr. Barry Sears
www.zoneperfect.com

Chapter 7

Dr. Mitchell E. Gibson

Dr. Mitchell E. Gibson is a board-certified forensic psychiatrist, author, astrological researcher, and public speaker. He is a diplomate of the American Board of Psychiatry and Neurology, the American College of Forensic Medicine, and the American Board of Forensic Examiners. Dr. Gibson is a former chief of staff at the East Valley Camelback Hospital, and he was chief resident in psychiatry at Albert Einstein Medical Center. He is a graduate of the University of North Carolina at Chapel School of Medicine. Dr. Gibson is the author of Signs of Mental Illness, the first astrological study of mental disease in history, and Signs of Psychic and Spiritual Ability, the first astrological study of paranormal phenomena. Dr. Gibson has completed work on two software packages based on his research, entitled Signs: The *Software* Spiritual Sky and Signs: The Inner Sky.

The Interview

David E. Wright (Wright)

Dr. Mitchell E. Gibson is a board-certified psychiatrist who has been in practice in the Tempe area for ten years. Dr. Gibson is a former chief of staff at the East Valley Camelback Psychiatric Hospital, and he was chief resident in psychiatry at the Albert Einstein Medical Center in Philadelphia. He has served as medical consultant for KPNX-TV 12 in Phoenix for seven years and KTAR 620 AM for eight years, and has made over three hundred radio and TV appearances. He also consults for a number of regional and national businesses, consumer magazines and newspapers, including *The Arizona Republic,* the *Mesa Tribune,* the *Arizona Business Gazette, Ebony, Essence,* and *Phoenix Magazine.*

Dr. Gibson is a graduate of the University of North Carolina at Chapel Hill, and he's also board certified in forensic medicine and forensic examination. He has twice been named to the Top Doctors list of *Phoenix Magazine* and to the Best Doctors of America compilation assembled by Woodward/White. Dr. Gibson is currently in private practice in Tempe, Arizona.

Dr. Gibson, welcome to *Mission Possible!*.

Dr. Mitchell Gibson (Gibson)
Good morning, David and Alex.

Alexandria Altman (Altman)
It's a pleasure to be interviewing you today.

Gibson
Thank you.

Wright
Dr. Gibson, in one of your articles you said that *Signs of Mental Illness* is a provocative new breakthrough in medicine and astrology. What do you mean?

Gibson

There is some research that I did over the last six years or so that looked at comparing the charts of people who have had serious recurring mental illness to the charts of people who have never had a diagnosis of mental illness and who by testing are considered mentally healthy. When you compare those two, you find that there are some astrological differences in how their planets are placed, so that just from their birth information, using a computer program that I've written, you can pick out a person's risk factor of what kind of mental illness they might develop and how serious it will be.

Altman

David, I had a chance to talk to Dr. Gibson before this interview. He has designed a great program. Can you tell us a little bit about how you designed the program and its availability to people?

Gibson

It is a program that was written in Windows. Basically, all you have to do is put in your birth information, and it gives you three types of reports. The first is just a one-page printout of your risk factors for different mental illnesses. The second level of report is a little more in-depth, and it gives you the astrological correlation to what those illnesses might be and how severe they might be. The third level of report is a twenty-page report that you can use in more depth. The program is a point-and-click, easy-to-use, Windows-driven program, and it works fantastically.

Wright

Is it for sale?

Gibson

It is for sale. You can find it at Amazon.com or you can get it through my office.

Altman

Is medicine and astrology linked together somehow, Dr. Gibson?

Gibson

Up until the early 1900s, medical schools taught astrology as part of their regular curriculum, which means that if you were in medical school, you had to take astrology. That is actually still true in some parts of the world. India, for instance, still requires that, as well as some parts of South America.

Wright

That's strange. I would suppose most of the public has no idea of that.

Gibson

It used to be that if you went to medical school, you had to study astrology. In Tibet, in your first year of medical school you take basic astrology as part of your first-year curriculum, and that's today.

Altman

Dr. Gibson, I've been in the ER a lot. I've heard nurses and doctors say, "There must be a full moon." That has a lot to do with this, doesn't it?

Gibson

The full moon has something to do with it. It does affect people's moods. When I was in the emergency room, when I was working in hospitals a lot, we always dreaded for a full moon to come up, because when the moon was full, we got more calls to the emergency room, the emergencies were worse, and people didn't get better as fast. It was a totally different interaction. And when the moon went off of being full, it was calmer, quieter, totally different.

Altman

Is it true that during a full moon is the worst time to have surgery?

Gibson

There is some clinical information to suggest that if you have surgery during a full moon, or have any procedure during a full moon, you're more likely to bleed, and there is a slightly increased risk of infection.

Altman

My grandmother used to say that, and I wondered if it was true.

Gibson

Yes, there is some research that would suggest that.

Wright

Dr. Gibson, could you tell us how Modern Astrology differs from traditional astrology?

Gibson

Modern Astrology is different from traditional astrology in that we don't use Sun Signs, which means that we don't really care if you were born as a Virgo, a Cancer, or a Capricorn. We don't use that at all. Also, we don't use the Ascendant or the Descendant or the Houses.

Altman

Can you give us an example of Modern Astrology?

Gibson

For instance, in Modern Astrology, if you want to get a reading, we take your regular birth information and use something called a multiple planet aspect, which means that you might take a grouping of three planets rather than just where the Houses are, and that says something about a person; or a grouping of five planets, if it's in a person's chart. That's called a plenary elevation, actually, and that says something about a person. That's not very common. So we tend to use the actual planetary position of the planets based on when a person was born and the traverse of what the planets are doing.

The problem with the House system and the old astrology system is that they are somewhat out of date. The earth has moved in its position on its axis. Also, it's moved relative to the constellations; so if you think you were born as a Virgo, you actually are astrologically a Leo. You look at what your sun is. If your birth chart says you are a Virgo, your sun is actually in Leo. You're actually the sign ahead of where you think you are.

Wright

Are you saying that people who are born under the same birth sign do not have similar characteristics?

Gibson

They do have similar characteristics, but the thing about birth charts and astrological signs is that a lot of people have those same characteristics, unfortunately.

Altman

So are you saying that you really aren't true to your sign according to your birth date?

Gibson

Everybody has some element of truth to their sign. There is some validity to working with the House system and with the general system of astrological constellations. But scientifically and technically, it's not accurate. When looking at the sky and a person says, "I was born in the constellation of Virgo," you ask what time they were born and look at the star charts and see that the sun was nowhere near Virgo at that time. That makes it inaccurate.

Altman

Dr. Gibson, tell us about your work in *Signs of Psychic and Spiritual Ability.*

Gibson

That one's a lot more fun. In that particular research study, I took well over two hundred people who had great spiritual ability, as you would measure from their life history—people like Nostradamus, who probably was one of the greatest seers of all time, and Edgar Cayce and Ogla Worrall, who was probably one of the greatest healers of all time, and Joan of Arc. I compared them to two hundred people who had no real differentiation from the masses as far as their psychic or spiritual potential. I compared the charts. From that system, I came up with a grouping of what I call "marker aspects." In this marker aspect system, an average person might have a score of between 50 and 100. That's pretty common. Somebody that is spiritually gifted can have a score as high as 300 or 400. My score in that system was 65, by the way. Nostradamus has a score of over 260. Joan of Arc's score is over 300. But the average person is nowhere near that. That's available in a program as well.

Wright

How are you defining "spiritual"? Is that belief in God?

Gibson

I broke the term "spiritual" down into four different categories. One is *general psychic ability*, the ability to have clairvoyance or telepathy or that sort of thing that you can do at a very high level of control. Another level is *psychic and spiritual healing*. These people make their living as healers who are very effective, even as tested by medical doctors. Another grouping has to do with people that we would call *mediums*. These people have the ability to work with intelligences that have passed on beyond the realm of death. The fourth is a group of people we call *mystics*—that refers to a certain level of soul development that allows them to communicate with God and different parts of themselves at such a high level that it can effect things that we call miracles.

Wright

There are two gentlemen on television right now who seem to be making a lot of money and doing a lot business getting in touch with people who have passed on. Do you see validity in that?

Gibson

You know, ten years ago I would have laughed at you and said, "That's a bunch of crap." But during my research for this book, I have met well over a hundred mediums, people who make their professional living doing this kind of work. I would say that out of those hundred mediums, there were about thirty of them that you just couldn't explain away. They were able to sit down with me and tell me things about people that I knew had passed away and that they should not have known. My grandmother, for instance—they knew about her life, what she died of, what she called me as my nickname, and what she looked like.

They were also able to tell me about a friend of mine who had died, who I wasn't even asking about. They said that he wanted to talk since I was communicating with the other side. They knew his name, which was very unusual. They knew how he died, what he looked like, and that he was not a very common-looking person. They consistently did that. So to me it says that there is something there, something that has survived, and there are certain individuals that this program can identify who can communicate with people.

Altman

That's incredible.

David, I had the pleasure of Dr. Gibson doing a very short reading for me, and what he does is extraordinary.

Gibson

David, would you like for me to see what your potential is?

Wright

Wait till I get to the racetrack and then I'll call you!

Dr. Gibson, with our *Mission Possible!* talk show and book, we are trying to encourage people in our audience to be better, live better, and be more fulfilled by listening to the examples of our guests. Is there anything or anyone in your life who has made a difference for you and helped you to be a better person?

Gibson

I would say my grandmother, for one. She was the person who convinced me actually to go to college. She talked me into it. I was going to join the Air Force. That's what the men in my family did— we went into the Air Force; we didn't go to college. She said, "You're bright and you deserve to have a college education." So I really have to credit her with changing the course of my entire life.

Then I had a college professor who, unfortunately, passed not too long ago. He was the first person who really took an interest in teaching me how to do research. Even though I didn't have any research experience, he gave me a job in his research lab. For the next two years, he taught me how to do chemistry research. It had a profound influence on the rest of my life. Since that time, I've really dedicated my life to doing a lot of different types of research. In my first professional exposure to research, I did papers and talks, research competitions, and I corresponded with labs and scientists around the world. I really have to credit him for that. Those two people were very influential in my life.

Wright

It's interesting; when Alex and I ask our guests about people who have made an impact on their lives, almost without exception they—and some books I have read say as high as eighty percent of all people—point to some teacher as a great mentor or someone who had a great impact on their life.

Gibson

I think teachers have a very unique position in society, inter-acting with young minds, in that they can recognize things about their students' mental and emotional capacity that maybe at a young age the students just don't see in the same way. In doing that, teachers can guide them in ways that they may never have thought about. It can profoundly alter their ideas about themselves, about the world, about what they are doing with their lives. It's just profoundly moving and fantastic what a good teacher can do. Before I met my college professor, I was not interested in research. It was not something I wanted to do. He really showed me it was something I had a talent for.

Altman

Dr. Gibson, what do you think makes up a great mentor? In other words, are there characteristics that mentors seem to have in common?

Gibson

I think a mentor is, more than anything, a patient person. I think mentors also have a keen interest in the people they are guiding. I think they have a certain amount of wisdom that is something above the ordinary. Not everybody can be a mentor. Not everybody can take a young mind and guide it and mold it in a way that a good mentor can. I think it's a skill.

I have my program up now. If you'd like, David, I can get your birth information and plug you in and see what kind of potentials you have.

Wright

Okay, I was born on March 11, 1939.

Gibson

Do you know what time?

Wright

I think I heard my mother say it was five o'clock in the afternoon.

Gibson

What city were you born in?

Wright

Knoxville, Tennessee.

Gibson

Okay, looking at your chart, your mystical potential is 180.

Wright

Is that good?

Gibson

That is the highest category. There are five categories: below average, which is 0 to 50; above average, which is 50 to around 100; superior, which is about 100 to 140; and outstanding, which is about 140 to 180. You're in the next category, which is the highest category, at 180. Your mystical potential is in the highest grouping. Healing is in the normal range—that's about 60. Psychic potential is in the outstanding range, at about 160, which is in the top ten percent of charts. Mediumship potential is slightly above average, but not nearly as high as psychic.

Wright

How do I develop any one of these characteristics?

Gibson

I think the one that might be best for you to develop would be psychic potential. Most people who have psychic potential don't know that they have it. They have slight twinges of intuition or elevated understanding. They might have some time when they can guess things that are going to happen, premonitions in the form of dreams. But without proper training, it will remain at that level. This is true even in people who have very high potential.

One thing I found in my research that was very consistent was that people with very well-developed ability also took the time to train it. Nostradamus had training, Edgar Cayce had training. Any of the people who were great in that area knew that they had potential and were wise enough to take the time to do some training. In Nostradamus's case, his father and grandfather trained him to be a seer.

In your case, one thing that would be useful for you to do would be to learn something called clairvoyant viewing, or remote viewing, usually the easiest and most satisfying psychic ability to develop initially. You can do that by going to a number of Web sites. Western Remote Viewing, out of Las Vegas, offers an excellent course in beginning clairvoyant remote viewing that is approached from a scientific standpoint. It allows you to use a very systematic, analytical, scientific technique to develop your psychic potential. You can check yourself along the way, no matter where you are starting, as far as your ability. As you develop, you can use the system to help yourself be challenged, and grow, regardless of what that ability is.

Wright

Dr. Gibson, of all the people I've read about or seen on television, Edgar Cayce was the only one that just fascinated me. Many, many years ago, I read everything I could get my hands on. What he was doing was so unique, and it fascinates me even to this day.

Gibson

Even someone with Edgar Cayce's ability would practice every day. Every day he would go into a trance and practice giving readings on people. Even though he was in a hypnotic trance while he was doing it, he still took the time every day to practice.

Altman

Dr. Gibson, when you pulled up my chart, you said, "There are only a couple of things that can stop you at success," and you told me what they were. Do you see anything in David's chart that would stop him from total success?

Gibson

One of the things we do in Modern Astrology is called a "temporal index"—temporal meaning time, and index relating to how fertile the time a person is born in. It's like taking a seed and planting it in the desert and watering it. I don't care what type or how fertile the seed is, you're putting it in bad soil. If you plant it in a good farm with an irrigation well, that seed is going to be more likely to grow. People are like that. If you take a person who is very gifted and give that person good parenting, a good school, a good diet, and good social interaction, that person is more likely to grow up to be successful.

The temporal environment is a measure of how likely a person is to have those things versus how much they are likely to struggle. There is an average range, below average, above average, outstanding, and a superior range. There are positive and negative ranges in all of that. Yours is slightly in the negative range, which means that you would have had much more of a tendency to struggle with life in general. Also, your negative karma is a little bit higher than normal.

Wright

Is there anything that can be done about that?

Gibson

I think the thing that would tend to be your biggest struggle is your Saturn-Mercury parallel in line with Neptune, which means that you really almost have to wrestle or struggle with your creative potential to make it do what you want it to do. Saturn is a planet of limitations and struggle. Mercury is a planet of creativity, communication, publishing, writing, radio, in particular. Neptune is a planet associated with the unconscious ideas, intuition. When you combine those three things together, it means you have to struggle to communicate your ideas that are creative and intuitive. Even though you have the potential, Mercury acts like a block that prevents you from getting those things out.

You also have the Sun-Jupiter eclipse, which is a very good eclipse to have. It means that you're very interested in those things and have a lot of fertile ideas, but you have to really work with the Saturn energy to get beyond that. Just because something might be difficult doesn't mean that you should stop. It means that the harder you push, the more likely you are to get what you want out of it. Those planets that I was talking about are in a very good place in your chart. They are in what we call the Ascendant, which is a place in the sky that predicts how successful a person might be. You have Saturn on the Ascendant; Mercury, the Sun, and Jupiter are within ten degrees of the Ascendant, which means that with enough work, you can accomplish pretty much what you want to, but you have to work at it.

Wright

Dr. Gibson, most people are fascinated with the new TV shows about being a survivor. What has been the greatest comeback you have ever made from adversity in your career or life?

Gibson

I would have to say from a very, very, very poor childhood. I grew up in a very poor town in rural North Carolina. We didn't have plumbing or electricity or telephone or anything until I was in high school. In the wintertime, if it was snowing outside, the temperature was the same inside as it was outside. I think overcoming that, just getting through that and getting into college, was a major accomplishment.

Altman

Dr. Gibson, would you like to give us a Web site for people if they want to contact you?

Gibson

I do have a Web site. It's www.modernastrology.com.

Altman

That's how they can reach you to get a reading, right?

Gibson

That's right. The reading lasts about an hour. There are two levels, basic and advanced. On a basic reading, you can ask any five questions you like about any particular topic you like. Most people like to ask about jobs and relationships, which is okay. You can also get a spiritual reading or mental health reading.

Altman

When you consider the choices you've made down through the years, has faith played an important role in your life?

Gibson

Yes, I think my faith in God and my faith in the fact that the universe is going to take care of me has been crucial in helping me get to where I am and staying there.

Wright

If you could have a platform and tell our audience something you think would help or encourage them, what would you say?

Gibson

If you have a dream, no matter what that dream is, don't let anything stop you from working your hardest and your best to get that dream. The only thing that can stop you is not working at it consistently. With determination, you can do just about anything you want to do.

Wright

That's sound advice.

This has been a very fast thirty minutes. We have been talking to Dr. Mitchell Gibson, who is a board certified psychiatrist who has been practicing for ten years in the Tempe, Arizona, area. Dr. Gibson, we really appreciate your being on our program today.

Gibson

Thank you for having me.

Mission Possible!

Altman

Thank you, Dr. Gibson.

Gibson

Thank you, Alexandria.

Mitchell E. Gibson, M.D.
Suite C-2, 2600 E. Southern Avenue
Tempe, Arizona 85282 USA
Telephone: 480.838.4300
Fax: 480.838.4200
mitchellgibson@worldnet.att.net
www.modernastrology.com

Chapter 8

Ty Boyd

Ty Boyd is unparalleled in the nation as a speaker and communications coach. He has delivered keynotes and conducted seminars on five continents to more than a million people. He is one of the few speakers worldwide to receive the speaking industry's three highest honors, including the "Oscar" of the National Speakers Association– The Cavett Award.

The Interview

David E. Wright (Wright)

We are speaking today with Ty Boyd. Ty has spent a lifetime learning the tools of the powerful communicator, tools that have made him a successful broadcaster, consultant, teacher, and internationally known professional speaker. Ty is past president of the four thousand member National Speakers Association, founder of the Excellence in Speaking Institute, and winner of three top awards in the speaking profession, including the "Oscar" of the National Speakers Association, the coveted Cavett Award. He is

also a member of the North Carolina Broadcasters Hall of Fame.
Thank you for being with us today, Mr. Boyd.

Ty Boyd (Boyd)

Dave, it's so great to be with you—and it's Ty, by the way.

Wright

Okay.

Boyd

You and I actually have connected many times in the past, so it's
just old friends.

Wright

I appreciate that. My first question to you is born out of curios-
ity. After all those years of traveling and speaking to people around
the world, how did you have the time to have six children?

Boyd

Well, you always have to come home and change clothes. I tell
you, we have the greatest relationship. Pat Boyd and I have been
married for forty-one years, and we've been partners for forty-one
years. We are in business together, and she and I travel a great deal
together. We have six children and several grandchildren, number-
ing eight, at this point. So my fellow player hasn't been too far away.

Wright

That's great.

Alexandria Altman (Altman)

During my research on your book, Ty, I saw where you spoke to
eighty thousand people at the Georgia Dome. Tell me how nervous
you were.

Boyd

Alexandria, I have spoken to a hundred and fifty audiences in a year and had not gotten up to eighty thousand. Audience sizes are different, but the dynamics are actually the same. The thing to do, first of all, is to connect with the audience, whoever it happens to be. (Believe me, I'm going to answer your question in a moment.) Second, it's just to consider it a conversation, a conversation with eighty thousand individuals, not a swarm of people. So it really is kind of one-on-one, magnified. We were at the Georgia Dome, and that happened to be a huge multilevel marketing meeting. George Bush, Sr., was also on the program. I tell you, he spoke for twenty minutes and got $100,000. I spoke for an hour; I'm not going to tell you what I got, but it certainly wasn't $100,000.

Altman

Maybe you should run for President and your salary would go up.

Boyd

I don't know. The President doesn't get but about $400,000 a year. Now that's a lot of money to some of us, but some speakers I know seem to get more than that.

Wright

Right. Ty, could you tell our listeners just how you decided to go into the speaking/training business? I know you were such a successful broadcaster. I read at one point in time that you were guest host for *The Arthur Godfrey Show*, weren't you?

Boyd

Yes, but that was a long time ago. I thought at that time broadcasting was the center of the universe. Of course, it still is a big part, but the old Ty Boyd focused a lot on himself. I really wanted to be a big star. My focus has changed. By the way, I believe the secret of real communication came to me after that stint, after that period in my life.

But you asked how I got involved with speaking. The truth is, every person who is listening this very minute is a professional speaker. It's not something some people do, it's something we all do—whether we're a Sunday school teacher or nurse or doctor or pilot or broadcaster or parent or teacher or preacher.

Let me tell you what we say about communication. We say it's the number one skill. Listen to me—this is what the professional speaker has to know, what the broadcaster knows; it's what the leader needs to know, the manager, salesperson, parent, spouse, teacher, minister, lover, lawyer. It's the thing that distinguishes who we are, what we are, and how effective we're going to be. It is the most "money" skill there is, the most valuable "relation" skill, the most powerful "success" skill that we have.

You asked me about being a broadcaster; I think I'm telling you what I have learned from the beginning as a broadcaster, and now as a teacher and working in life skills.

Altman

Has raising your children been a lot easier because you are a professional communicator?

Boyd

I'm not sure whether is has been or not, Alexandria. I don't know what it's like not to be a fairly good listener and fairly articulate. Our relationship with our family has always been just fabulous. Parents do have blind spots, and children do have times they'd like to be without their parents, but we've had a fabulous relationship.

Altman

Ty, how many of your six children do you think will follow in your shoes professionally?

Boyd

We have three of them in broadcast right now. It is so gratifying to their father. Actually, four or five . . . well, all of them, have had a taste of it in one way or another. Two work for us in our business. Our oldest was the news director for the top-rated station here in Charlotte, Lite102.9. Anne Cowden Boyd is one of our lead instructors. And if you call our office, you'll most probably get Molly Boyd on the phone, or an equally lovely lady named Sheila Adams. Molly has worked for us the last couple of years, and she has the most incredible relationship skills you've ever seen.

Wright

That's great. By the way, I read your book that's hot off the press. I'd like to plug it, if you don't mind. It's called *The Million-Dollar Toolbox: A Blueprint for Transforming Your Life and Your Career with Powerful Communication Skills.* I notice that both you and your wife wrote it.

Boyd

Pat and I work together, though my name is on most of the work we do. You and Alexandria know this. It's not a one-person job. There's team involvement in almost every success, and certainly we've been a team; she is as equally responsible as I.

This is how the book came about. I am not an action-oriented person too often. I love to plan and get good ideas and feel very creative, but, somehow, executing them is quite difficult for me. Pat is the one who kept saying, "We've got to write the book. We've got to write the book." And so it came about.

We had a training company which we called Executive Learning Systems. We taught thousands of executives from over thirty countries, from every state in the union and every province in Canada. We taught them communication skills and how to be more effective communicators. If that's the number one skill, the people who are more successful are the ones who can communicate with their customers, both internal and external—internal meaning your family, the people you work with, that sort of thing, and external meaning the people who buy your services or to whom you render services. They're the ones who are most effective in communicating with those people. It doesn't mean being perfect. It doesn't mean being the best in the whole world. It's doesn't mean every time you stand up that people will say, "Wow!" or "Oh!"—sometimes the most effective communication is listening. So we've been teaching executives how to be more effective as communicators, listeners, leaders, managers, and sales people—that sort of thing.

Wright

I was impressed with your marketing skills when I looked on the dustcover of your hardback book and noted that you were at least intelligent enough to put a good-looking woman's picture on it, right?

Boyd

Listen, those are my hormones speaking. Forty years ago, when I saw that incredible lady, I said, "She's got to be a part of my future, even if it takes marrying her."

Wright

One of your friends told me that she was a beauty queen.

Boyd

She was, and she had much more celebrity than I when we were married. I was a young disc jockey in Chapel Hill, North Carolina, and did a local dance party not unlike Dick Clark's. Pat was a celebrity. She had been the National Maid of Cotton. She moved from there to be a Candy Jones model in New York, and she happened to be in the Chapel Hill–Durham area one summer as a celebrity and star. I had her on the television program, and we met there. We've been dating ever since.

Wright

That's great. Do you mind if I ask you some questions about your book?

Boyd

As long as you don't ask me how old she is!

Wright

Trust me, I will not. When people say, "Ty is a natural," or "I'll never be that good in a million years," or "He was born with speaking talent," what do you tell them?

Boyd

Well, it is true that some people just seem to be naturals. I mean, Michael Jordan is a natural. But he never would have been a "great" had he not worked on those skills with more dedication than you or I would care to put into most of our endeavors. So it is true, some people are blessed with more athletic talent, with the ability to use their bodies more effectively. But the truth is, every person who is listening right now, every person, not leaving a soul out—every man, woman, and child from every background, from every level of education, from every ethnicity—we all have all the tools, if we work hard enough, to be the Michael Jordan of communication, or the Tiger Woods, or the Jack Nicklaus, or the Barry Bonds.

Altman

Ty, what is your favorite chapter in your book, and could you elaborate on it?

Boyd

I would say . . . gosh, that's hard. I'm going to tell you that I think the first chapter is really powerful because it demystifies what we do. Looking at contemporary people, if you look at broadcasters, some of them are great at focusing on themselves and being somewhat articulate, but they do not make effective talk show hosts, because successful talk show hosts have a different sort of skill. They have to be able to listen much more effectively.

Altman

How large a part does charisma play in communication?

Boyd

It's a huge tool. It's just one of the tools, but there are people who seem to have a lot of, as Roger Ailes says, "likeability" about them. They are people that you really want to be with, that you really want to be around. Don't you have people in your life like that?

Altman

Certainly I do.

Boyd

And by the way, the same people would not attract everyone. What's attractive to you or me may not be attractive to someone else. But charisma is a powerful tool. That's the ability to make other people feel pretty good about themselves while they also feel mighty good about you. Charisma has to be authentic. A lot of people are attractive until you get up close. A lot of people are charismatic and attractive, but fall short when it comes to being able to trust them, for example. So charisma really measures through a lot of different levels. Would you agree with that?

Wright

Yes, I would.

Altman

I would too. You remind me of someone who has a magnetic personality.

Boyd

You're nice to say that. I'd like to agree with you, but what I think makes a person more powerful and creates charisma is to be able to be authentic—that's finding out who you really are and letting that be your filter, letting that be the way you live. But it also means being vulnerable. And the more vulnerable you are, the more people are going to like you and want to be around you, but you also leave yourself open to hurt, to surprises. However, I believe it's better to pay the price to be surprised or disappointed every once in a while than to try to be somebody you're not.

Wright

I didn't discuss this with Alexandria, but a few years ago at a meeting in Atlanta, Georgia, with nine hundred people, most of whom were professional speakers, I remember thinking how easily you put us all at ease from the very beginning of your presentation. You told a story that actually brought laughter, gales of laughter, from nine hundred men and women. We laughed for three or four minutes. It seemed to me like an eternity.

Boyd

I don't remember ever being that funny, David, but I may have been. I may have spoken after the cocktail party.

Wright

You also did something else that I appreciated. You gave someone else all of the credit for the story that you told.

Boyd

Aren't those all relationship tools that we have? I have a man who recently . . . and I say this not to tell you that I have a building named after me, but I have a very good friend who is several years younger than I, and I was his mentor when he first got into broadcast. Well, he's made lots of money and has been very successful. He's a powerful communicator and has built several buildings, huge office buildings worth millions and millions of dollars, and he named one of them Boyd Hall.

Altman

Oh, how great! That is wonderful.

Boyd

And what I've always said about Jim Heavener, the man who did that, is some people are very successful, then they run around trying to find someone to give credit to. I believe giving credit to other people is wonderful; everybody wins. Too often we're saying, "Hey, everybody, look at me." If we could focus on other people, as communicators we would be far less threatening to them and far more effective. May I give you a quote? Dale Carnegie, who's one of my heroes in communications and broadcast, said, "You can make more friends in two months by becoming interested in other people than you can in two years by trying to get other people interested in you." So anyway, I think it has everything to do with where we focus. The secret of life is to find out the wonderful payback in focusing on others.

Wright

Expanding on the communication topic, for the people in our audience who simply want to be heard or understood by their family, friends, or co-workers, what do you say to them?

Boyd

Good question; very good question, and a complex one. I'll give you a quick answer, but I think we could make that one question the topic of the whole program. First of all, I have found that some people are just talkers, like me, and they have to learn with adaptive behavior how to listen. It's very difficult to get other people always to do things exactly the way you'd like them to. But a quick answer to your question: If we will first listen to others, dignify others, and then proceed to talk, and if we are respectful of them, they should be respectful of us and allow us to express our ideas. That doesn't always happen short-term, but if we do it enough with family members, with fellow associates, with customers, with listeners on the radio, they will give us equal respect and speak to us and allow us to communicate and help us to feel more a part of the dialogue. But I'm taking too many words to answer a wonderful question.

Wright

Has faith been important to you in your career?

Boyd

Faith is a huge part of my life, especially in the trying times that our country finds ourselves in now. We have to search for an answer and look for help. The truth is, every day we use God as our co-pilot, we have a much lighter load. I read that humorous but wonderful signage recently which said, "You can relax today, everything is in My hands, signed God." That's kind of the way it went. And the truth is, we can all use that kind of support. It doesn't mean that all of our cares and troubles go away. I would have a difficult time always maintaining a good attitude if I didn't have my faith. Going back a little farther in my life, I would say that I took a lot for granted and have had to come through my own explorations and need to depend so much on my faith as a powerful support and leadership and bright light for me.

Wright

Let me change the subject for just a minute. Ty, the purpose of this program and a subsequent book is to help people do better and live more fulfilled lives. We hope that the examples of our successful guests, like you, will help in this goal. In this connection, has adversity played an important part in your life and career?

Boyd

Don't we learn our greatest lessons through adversity? If a thing is too easy, we tend not to take many lessons from it except that the easy way is the best way, and that quite often is not necessarily the case or the lesson we need to learn. Yes, I've learned a lot through adversity. I say in the book *The Million-Dollar Tool Box* that one of the most excruciatingly painful broadcast interviews I ever did was with Jonathan Winters, who is one of the funniest men on the face of this globe, and maybe in outer space too. I tried to be funny with him and match his wit, and he became terribly sober in our conversation. It was the most painful thing I've ever done, but I learned when not to compete with another guy on his turf.

Wright

It's been said by more than one person that he and Robin Williams are the two geniuses in that field.

Boyd

They are two huge talents and geniuses, no question. I don't know whether they are the only two, but they are fabulous.

Wright

I realize this question might be outdated by the time people read this book or by the time they listen to this interview, but in general terms, realizing what has happened in the last few weeks in the New York bombings and subsequent events, what do you think of all that's happened?

Boyd

I will just give you a layman's comment. I'm not qualified to answer that question except to tell you my own personal feelings and experience. I am devastated, numb, unsure of my ultimate thoughts, but the terror of September 11 has caused me to do several things. One, to appreciate my country more than ever, to love my fellowman more than ever, and to help me decide what is really important in life. Second, it has been to me a wake-up call: "Ty, in life, just as in communication, it isn't all about you. It's about you and others, so you'd better not monologue; you'd better dialogue." And though I think we are justified in doing everything we've done since September 11, I would say it's a great call to learn to listen to the rest of the world. If the rest of the world is determined that we are, for whatever reason, exemplary of the bad guy, then we need to know why they think that.

Altman

So you think communication skills could have helped in this situation?

Boyd

I'm going to say lack of communication is a big part, a big play, and that's over decades, particularly the last twenty or thirty years. Since the Second World War, which is over fifty years ago, I would say that we haven't been too interested in the rest of the world. We have had such a fabulous ride here creating this incredible democracy that I love so much, that we may be guilty of not having listened to the rest of the world as we could have, and as I hope we will. It doesn't mean that they are the good guys and we're the bad, or that they're right and we're wrong, or vice versa. It simply means that dialogue is so critically important now, and it is forever. It has moved from fester to fight.

Wright

I personally have listened to, read more, and asked more questions about a different lifestyle and a different religious attitude than I've ever been interested in before, and I'm learning things in a variety of ways, from my Sunday school class to the Internet. I'm learning a lot about people that I knew absolutely nothing about before. Perhaps some good can come from all this.

Boyd

Likewise. That area of the world is absolutely a dark place in terms of my enlightenment. So I, too, just as you, am going to learn much more about that part of the world. This has forced me to do so.

Wright

I have really, really enjoyed talking to you, Ty. You are one of my favorite people.

Boyd

Dave, I want to give your audience something that I haven't given them. Would that be possible?

Wright

Fine, but also I want you to give them some information. Perhaps a telephone number that they can call to purchase your book. I do believe that they can really change their life for the better, and *Transforming Your Life* is a good subtitle for this book.

Boyd

We believe so. We've put twenty-one years into creating the contents of this book and working with executives from every walk of life. If I were giving your listeners, right this minute, about three or four ideas, the first would be this: The greatest tool that we have is our energy and our passion. People with fire in their bellies get things done, and when they speak we listen. People who are just fact-based—and facts are critically important, but if we could take our facts and create a story, becoming more passionate and energetic, with fire in our bellies for our topic, others will hear it in a different way than they've ever heard before. So I'd say, work on listening. Gosh, I'm back where I'd like to be for interview number two. There is so much I'd like to say about the contents of this book. It's so powerful to take ordinary daytime tools and make them the tools of leaders and giants and lovers and great communicators.

Altman

Ty, you sound like a great storyteller. I could listen to you the rest of the afternoon.

Boyd

Stories are a powerful tool. Jesus spoke in parables. Mohammed spoke in parables. Martin Luther King spoke in parables. Billy Graham speaks in parables. Jack Welch, General Electric, speaks maybe not in parables but in storytelling. It's a great skill.

Wright

Well, do you have a telephone number that we might put in our book and in this interview so that our readers and listeners can order this book?

Boyd

You bet. People can learn more about the book and get a lot of free stuff, by the way. They can extract a chapter from the book and a lot of other free things. They can download a lot of stuff from our Web site, which is www.tyboyd.com. They can also buy the book at our Web site, or they can call us at our toll-free number, 800.336.2693. And you're just really great to let me come and chat with you on your program.

Wright

Well, Ty, we really enjoyed it. Alexandria and I learn more every time we talk to somebody like you, and we really do appreciate it.

Boyd

Let me congratulate you on being really outstanding listeners. And when you get a talker like me, your skill is really needed; too few of us do it very well.

Altman

Thank you so much. We definitely all need *The Million-Dollar Toolbox* here. Thank you for writing it.

Wright

We've been talking today with Ty Boyd. See you next time.

Ty Boyd
800.336.2693
www.tyboyd.com

Chapter 9

Frank Weldon

Frank Weldon, Master Certified Coach, professional speaker, and trainer, is one of the pioneers of executive coaching. He currently speaks to and trains professionals throughout the United States, Australia, and the United Kingdom on leadership, team synergy, and harnessing creativity in business.

The Interview

David E. Wright (Wright)

Today we are talking to Frank Weldon, certified coach, professional speaker, and trainer. As an international speaker with experience on three continents, Frank demonstrates that leadership principles work equally well in business and family. Frank, welcome to *Mission Possible!*.

Frank Weldon (Weldon)

Thank you, David.

Alexandria Altman (Altman)

Welcome, Frank.

Weldon

Thank you, Alex.

Wright

Frank, as I read your background and accomplishments, I couldn't help but be intrigued by the fact that you almost became an Episcopal priest. Could you tell us about that?

Weldon

Certainly. It may not be what you expect, though. I look at that era of my life as my first death and resurrection. Should I explain that a little bit?

Wright

I wish you would.

Weldon

I grew up in an alcoholic family and had a lot of anger. I was also a Catholic and had a lot of rules and commandments, and that was a pretty lethal combination for me. So when I was in college, I had a born-again experience and discovered that God was a loving God, not a judging God. But I still had a lot of anger and a lot of shame. When I was looking to see what I wanted to do with my life, I wanted to become an Episcopal priest, because I wanted to share the message of God's love.

The reason that I was "almost" a priest was that anger and shame still pretty much ran me while I was in seminary. I wasn't aware of it. If you had asked me at the time, I could have given you an argument about how it was everybody else's fault, they didn't understand me there, and those kinds of things. I wasn't recommended for ordination because of the anger and shame that they saw, which I didn't see at the time. My identity was caught up in being a priest, and I thought that was what God was leading me to be. So when that fell apart for me, it was like a death. It was the worst thing I could possibly imagine happening. As a matter of fact, I didn't imagine it happening. When it did happen, it was the most horrible experience I had had in my life. Yet as I look back on it, that is what it took for me to begin the healing that had to happen. So that is why I call it a death and resurrection. Have you heard of "the dark night of the soul"?

Altman

Oh, yes.

Weldon

Well, there was no dark night of the soul for me; it was a dark decade. It took about ten years, but it was really what launched my spiritual journey in more depth and taught me some humility as well.

Wright

When you say "they" kept you out of the priesthood, who are "they"? Was it the people at the university?

Weldon

No, it was the University of the South, in your part of the country. At the end of your seminary career, there is a formal process where they tell you whether or not they are going to recommend to your bishop that you be ordained. I was not recommended for ordination. It's funny, because I had another bishop from another diocese ask me to join his diocese right before that, so I found myself in a new diocese where I didn't have any friends who knew me. I didn't understand about politics and people, and it was almost like God shot down every possibility for me to be a priest at that time. Looking back, it was painful. But that's what I needed in order to start my healing.

Soon after that I started going to Al-Anon. (This was before Adult Children of Alcoholics existed.) I started dealing with my own victimization. It is said, David, that you should teach what you most know. I found out nobody really wanted a seminar on how to be a victim and how to manipulate other people's lives with your own victimization, but I could certainly teach that course.

Wright

You and I have similar backgrounds as far as alcohol in our family is concerned. One of the problems I had for many years was that I felt hurt, shame, and many other things. I thought being an alcoholic was just a lack of character. Back that many years ago, we didn't realize it was a disease. It sure did help me understand my father when I found out it was a disease, when I was in my twenties or thirties.

Weldon

That's about how old I was. I was in my twenties and thirties when this was happening. I also came to realize that every one of us is addicted to something.

Altman

That's true. We all have some little skeleton in our closet that wants to poke its head out now and then.

Weldon

I've come to look at addictions as those substances we consume or those behaviors that we do in order not to feel our pain. I was never addicted to any substances, but I was addicted to spending and credit cards at one time in my life. Trust me, behaviors can be addicting as well. If I was feeling some emotional pain, instead of dealing with the pain I would go shopping. Do you follow me?

Wright

Yes, except now you are preaching and meddling at the same time.

Weldon

Right. What I've discovered is I can walk through the pain with the help of God. One of the things about those death-and-resurrection moments is that you don't see any hope. You're doing the best you can. You're doing everything you know how to do. You realize how inadequate you are, and it seems hopeless. I've been brought into those situations several times in my life. That's when faith comes in. That's when you go on, even though you don't see any hope. And you pray. Then somehow circumstances change or something shows up to give you a little bit of hope.

Those moments have become the most important moments of my life. May I share another one with you?

Wright

Certainly.

Weldon

It took me several years to really find myself after that. Trust me, my identity was caught up in being a priest, so I had no clue as to what to do next. I went through several sales jobs, but they didn't quite fit. Then I became a legal assistant and began to work in corporate America. I started to get some stability in my life, which was the next stage.

I remember driving home one time from working in a fairly high-pressure environment, and the shame that ran me. It was a rough day at work. I don't remember the details; I just remember the traffic was normal for Houston—horrible. By the time I got home, I was a volcano about to explode. My son was only four years old at the time. He did something that was probably true to form for a four-year-old, but I remember that it was the straw that broke the camel's back. I exploded and raged at him. All of a sudden, in the middle of that explosion and rage, I thought, "Frank, what are you doing? This is your son. He is one of the most important people in the world to you. There is nothing that he could have done to elicit that kind of reaction."

I remember going outside, separating myself for a while, and praying. It was one of those moments that in Christianity is referred to as "being convicted of your sinfulness." I've got to tell you, I have a chip on my shoulder about preachers who try to shame other people into salvation. But I was truly looking at what I had done to my son, not what my father had done to me, and I realized that I had become the monster. Once again it was one of those death-and-resurrection moments. I was able to move back from that, talk to my wife about it, and get some help to learn to deal with the rage and let it go. It's still there. I could still go there, but I don't.

Wright

Frank, you stated in your bio that your life turned around in 1986 when you became a paralegal and entered the corporate world. What really caught my attention was something you wrote, and this is a direct quote: "I also experienced the healing and growth that occurs when you work for a true leader." Can you talk about that?

Weldon

Absolutely. I'm talking about a man by the name of Ken Keener. As you know, David, what I teach right now as a speaker and trainer is leadership principles in families and leadership principles in business. They are the exact, same principles. I remember several incidents in different sales jobs. I'm a natural contributor, so I would say, "Hey, what if we do this?" I was always told to shut up, that I was there to do the work, and the thinking should be left to them. By the time I got to Ken Keener, I was still pretty broken. I remember a time when Ken called me in and said . . . well, let me back up just a second.

During orientation, there is a time when a new employee will ask a lot of questions. That time for me had really gone on longer than usual, and I was having Ken do my work for me. I would come to him with questions about things that were really mine to do, but I was so afraid of taking risks that I was pushing it all off on him. What he did at that time was say, "You know, we hired you because you are smart, and I really think you can come up with a better solution to this particular problem than I can. As a matter of fact, in the future, when you've got a problem, why don't you investigate two or three solutions, bring them to me, and then I'll decide. Recommend the solution you would take and tell me why."

So I started doing that. In the beginning he had one or two responses. One response was, "Looks good to me; go do it." Usually he would follow my recommendations. However, since his knowledge and experience were greater than mine, at other times he would ask me questions. After a while, his universe of understanding about my job and my universe of understanding were about the same, and I noticed that he always took my recommendations. Some of those things were his decision to make.

I would make the recommendations, but they were his level, his decision to make. Other decisions were mine to make, but I would inform him. So other than for his decisions, it was an abuse of his time for me to tell him about it. But the thing about Ken was he made it safe for me to make mistakes. He used those as opportunities to "grow" me and teach me.

He did another thing later on. I was supposed to do a report that went to the CEO of the company. Ken was a lawyer. He was the one in charge of litigation for a Fortune 50 company. I was supposed to look around for all the different attorneys' fees in the company. We did this report on a quarterly basis, and we had just handed in the report for the first quarter. Right after that, I discovered another area of the company that also hired attorneys, and I found out that we had underreported attorneys' fees by a quarter of a million dollars. I walked into Ken's office fully expecting to be fired. I said, "Ken, I don't know how to tell you this, but you need to know. We've underreported. I've found these attorney fees." He saw how ashamed and frightened I was, and he said, "First of all, everybody makes mistakes. Second, we put you on this project because we felt you would be better at coming up with these different pockets of attorney fees than anyone else. And third, you're not going to make this mistake again, are you?" I remember walking into his office thinking I was going to get fired, and walking out on air.

Wright

That's a great leader, isn't it?

Weldon

Absolutely. The thing about Ken is that I wasn't the only one. He used to work for another company, and when we would travel together to go to depositions, every time we were in an airport one of his former employees would find him, come up to him, and say, "Mr. Keener, it is so good to see you."

Altman

That sounds great. Frank, what information are you getting to the people out there that will change them for the better?

Weldon

As I said, mostly I teach on leadership. The difference between a leader and a businessperson is that a businessperson is there to get results for the stockholders and for the business. Often those same businesspeople accomplish that at the expense of their employees. A leader is someone whom other people want to follow and feel safe enough to follow. So I let people know that yes, results are important, and strategies are important. A leader needs to understand that tools, time management, asset management, and strategies are all important, but they are not everything. A leader knows how to work with people, how to be respectful of them.

It's funny how most of us like to think of ourselves as respectful, but when we get tied to the work, we lose sight of being respectful to others, and we start yelling at other people like I yelled at my son that day. We need to be respectful of other people; we need to find a way that they can benefit from the work as well as our company benefiting from the work. Ken groomed me. It was an incredible experience working for him. I would seek him out at the coffeepot, because he was not only my boss, he was my friend.

The other thing that Ken had and that we need is integrity. One of the traps we fall into is this: Let's say I'm your boss, Alex. I'm going to expect you to keep your word to me, but often bosses don't realize they need to keep their word to the employee also.

Altman

That's correct. Integrity is the number one thing in my book.

Weldon

Absolutely. When I teach people, I do an exercise with them and ask them, "What do you want in your ideal boss?" We then come up with a list of qualities. About ten percent of these qualities are about result skills, and ninety percent about understanding and being respectful with people and about integrity.

Altman

Frank, with our *Mission Possible!* talk show and book, we are trying to encourage people in our audience to be better, live better, and be more fulfilled by listening to the examples of our guests. Is there anything or anyone in your life who has made a difference for you and helped you to be a better person?

Weldon

Bunches, Alex. Ken is one, obviously. There was another man I worked for at the same company by the name of Dwayne Emert. Dwayne was committed to his people. He wasn't as good of a communicator as Ken. He wasn't as good at creating safety. As a matter of fact, working for him I always felt like I was being thrown into deep water, and I didn't think I'd be able to swim. But one day he said to me, "You know, I don't give you a lot of instructions when I give you an assignment." I thought to myself, That's the truth. Then he said, "The reason I do that is that I don't want to stifle your creativity, and so far you have never let me down." He placed value in growing his people, but he had a different style, and he affected me.

There was also an Episcopal priest by the name of Father Hubbell. He was kind of an oddball for a priest, but he, too, was a loving, caring man, and he created safety for his people. I get mad at preachers who are constantly shaming people.

Altman

I think we all do.

Weldon

He didn't say he had all the answers, but he showed us love and care, and he had a profound effect on me.

Wright

Frank, in that connection, what do you think makes up a great mentor? In other words, are there characteristics that mentors seem to have in common?

Weldon

Yes. I make a distinction between a mentor and a coach, so let me make that distinction first. A coach is someone who is supposed to guide and direct individuals or a team toward specific goals. A mentor is someone who is just there to help. For a coach, the agenda is already set, but a mentor is someone who stands next to you and helps clear the path in front of you. Every good coach is also a mentor, but not every mentor is a coach, because they don't have that specific goal they are going after. But once again, it is about noticing when the student is ready, making it safe for the student to admit when help is needed, then, once that opening is there, showing the student something.

When I was coaching people, probably two-thirds of the time I spent with them was about making the message safe—making it safe to bring up emotionally sensitive information. Perhaps they were doing something that they were not aware they were doing, or some attitude they had was causing them problems. How was I to make it safe enough to show them where their actions or attitudes were creating the problem? A mentor or coach will show people that they are the problem in a safe enough way so they can say, "Yes, I see it now." And once they can see it, the coach or mentor says, "And here's an alternative."

So to me, one of the characteristics of a mentor is they can see the pattern and the problem. They are also aware that they can create enough safety to get that message through, and they have the skills to show the people they are mentoring a better way.

Altman

Thank you for clarifying that for us.

When you consider the choices you have made down through the years, has faith played an important role in your life?

Weldon

Yes, faith has played an important part. Once again, the faith that is most important to me is that faith when I just don't see a way out.

Something happened a couple of days ago, and I am so truly grateful that I have this kind of relationship with my son. My older son, the four-year-old that I mentioned previously, is now twenty. He has been having some girlfriend problems, and the other day after coming home from college on Christmas vacation he spoke with me. He has seen that, although it isn't his intention, he has some behaviors that are hurting people very badly, emotionally hurting them—people who are very important to him. He was looking in the face of his own sinfulness, if you will. He said, "Dad,

I don't see a way out. This is all I know how to be. I've been this way for thirteen or fourteen years. I don't see any hope." I said, "That's the time to pray."

I then shared with him some of the times my wife and I have had in our relationship. Now, we're like the Huxtables on the old *Cosby Show*, almost syrupy-sweet happy. It's almost embarrassing, but we haven't always been that way. We've been in that place where no matter what we did, we didn't see a way to continue our relationship. We've had several dark nights of the soul—those deaths, as I call them. The thing is, I have now had enough of those deaths and resurrections that I know something will come. God will send an answer, even though I don't know the answer right now. To me, that's what faith is.

Wright

Frank, let me ask you to go back, just for my benefit. I put a lot of faith in the meaning of words. Several times you used the word "safe" or "safety." Is that the antithesis of fear, as you use it?

Weldon

It's funny, David. I believe all behavior that is damaging ultimately is a result of fear. I wouldn't have thought of it that way, but yes, faith is the antithesis of fear. It's moments of faith, moving forward even though it looks hopeless. There is also confidence. I remember the last time my wife and I had some difficulties several years ago, there was a strange confidence. I was hurting, she was hurting, and yet we knew we had been through that before, and we knew we could make it again. That's confidence to me. But that real deep faith is when you don't see a way through it, but you keep going anyway, and you keep praying.

Wright

Most people are fascinated with the new TV shows about being a survivor. What has been the greatest comeback you have made from adversity in your career or life?

Weldon

I think I mentioned it earlier. My whole life has been a journey of healing. It started with coming to grips with the fact that I had a problem. My father had a drinking problem, but I had a victim problem. And I had a revenge and an anger problem. So it's been one continuous evolvement away from that brokenness to actually being happy and liking life. I feel so richly blessed. Along the way, there have been times when I've been laid off and I've been fired and different things have happened to me. Yet the big one was the seminary, because my identity was tied up in it.

Altman

Frank, you've explained faith really well for us. If you could have a platform and tell our audience something you believe would help or encourage them, what would you say?

Weldon

Jesus said, "The two greatest commandments are to love God with your whole heart, whole soul, and whole mind, and to love your neighbor as yourself." One of the things that I usually tell people, because it's in the realm of leadership and team development, is that we all have a choice between ego and spirit. We all have a choice between me and us. Us includes me, but me—that selfishness—doesn't include us. Me is a way to loneliness, and us is a way to happiness. Living in such a way that we all win creates a great result. That's what I think I would share.

Wright

In closing, I'd like to ask you a question. I've been working for churches for many years. How do you think the modern churches are doing nowadays?

Weldon

The modern churches? That's hard to say. Sometimes I love them, and sometimes I'm just furious with them. I believe if we could get back to the message of Jesus, of love and sharing and following what the Spirit tells us, we'd do much better. Sometimes we fall into the trap of thinking that now that we've been saved, we get to judge everyone else. It reminds me of two priests who worked at a church I used to attend. One priest was not nearly as confident, and he shared about love and life and said, "I don't have the answers." The other priest told me one time that he used to work at another church where he picked out the enthusiastic members and made them act like proper Episcopalians. Those are examples of both kinds of ministers in churches. The first I will follow; the second, I get angry with because they, in the name of Jesus, decide who to accept and who not to accept.

Wright

This has been a fast thirty minutes, and we're going to have to wrap it up. We've been talking to Frank Weldon, a certified coach, professional speaker, and trainer. He speaks internationally and has experience on three continents. He demonstrates leadership principles that work equally as well in business as in family. As you can tell by our interview, he has some great thoughts about how our families can live better lives. Frank, we really appreciate your visit to *Mission Possible!*.

Altman

This has been a really heartwarming experience. Thank you, Frank.

Weldon

Thank you, Alex. Thank you, David. I'm moved as I talk, and I thank you for the experience.

Wright

You're welcome. Maybe we can get together again some day.

Frank Weldon
Encouraging Words
Telephone: 281.463.2551
frankweldn@aol.com

Chapter 10

Rev. Dr. Erwin Deiser

Erwin Deiser is an ordained minister of Religious Science, teaching Science of Mind. He is the founder/pastor of Religious Science of Pembroke Pines, Florida, and the president of Have You Hugged Yourself Today, Inc. He earned a doctorate of chiropractic from Columbia Institute of Chiropractic in New York City and presently conducts workshops and seminars on a regular basis. He has been on radio and TV and proudly carries the titles "Hugman" and "Irreverent Reverand," given him due to his unique teaching style, which he calls Life Lessons, with practical spirituality as the base.

The Interview

David E. Wright (Wright)

Today we are talking to Erwin Deiser, an ordained minister of Religious Science. He is the founder of Religious Science of Pembroke Pines, Florida, and the president of Have You Hugged Yourself Today, Inc. He has held memberships in the National

Speakers Association and Florida Speakers Association, and he currently holds membership in the International Speakers Network. He is actively involved in Toastmasters International. Dr. Deiser earned a doctorate of chiropractic from Columbia Institute of Chiropractic (now New York College of Chiropractic) and actively conducts workshops and seminars. He has been on radio and television and proudly carries the titles "Hugman" and "Irreverent Reverend," given him due to his unique teaching style, which he calls Life Lessons, with practical spirituality as the base.

Dr. Deiser, welcome to *Mission Possible!*.

Deiser

Thank you; it's my pleasure.

Altman

Welcome, Dr. Deiser.

Deiser

Thank you.

Wright

Dr. Deiser, according to our research, you are training people to condition their minds or get their thoughts in line with their goals. Tell us, is controlling one's mind hard to do?

Deiser

Yes and no, David. First, we advise them that everything is mental—no exceptions. I don't train people to condition their minds. My goal is to help students recognize that the minds they are so proud of haven't been theirs for many years. Psychology recognizes that children's basic personalities are almost completed between one and seven years of age. Consciously or subconsciously, we are provided with concepts of others at a time when our minds are like sponges. We pick up our thinking from family, friends, teachers, and the world around us. We think we are expressing our own thoughts, but that isn't true. We have accepted a composite of thoughts on religion, race, society, individuals, and so forth, so our first task is to suggest to the students that they're working from anything but their own minds. I teach them that no matter what the source of their thinking may be, they are still responsible for the results of that thinking. I tell them that by changing their thinking they can change their lives. I teach them to recognize the mindset they are working from—not what to think, but how to think, how to use the most powerful instrument in the universe, mind power.

Wright

Are you saying we can change our lives by altering the way we think?

Deiser

Yes. The perfect example is the terrorist act of September 11. While the attack and destruction are incredibly tragic, the greatest tragedy is that a few dedicated people have been able to change the consciousness of our nation and the world. We have allowed them to take up residence in our minds. We need to evict them and take back our minds, individual by individual, in order to restore ourselves to the consciousness that prevailed prior to the tragedy of 9-11. We have become terrorists in our own minds.

Altman

Erwin, is that what the anthrax scare is all about?

Deiser

Fear. There has been so much on TV, radio, and in the newspaper about anthrax and its dire consequences if an individual is exposed to it—day after day, hour after hour, minute after minute, ongoing discussions of anthrax. It's not a wonder that so many people have accepted the fear of the consequences of anthrax, yet they may never be exposed to it. Some are afraid to come out of their homes, shop in a mall, even open their mail. The terrorists did their jobs well. They accomplished what they set out to do, which was to create fear, panic, and chaos. They have gotten into our minds. One commentator stated it well: "America will never be the same again." Roosevelt stated it differently many years ago: "We have nothing to fear but fear itself." We must get back to whatever is normal for each one of us. We need to be more aware of what is going on around us but get over our fears and move forward.

Altman

Erwin, are our relationships with others critical to our well-being or simply good for business and good for our personal lives?

Deiser

Relationships exist on many levels. Webster's definition says a relationship is connection by blood, marriage, or simply being related. If your validity is determined by a relationship, then, obviously, relationships will represent a critical aspect of your life. I would rather you review how you feel about your most important relationship, the one you are having with yourself. How do you feel about yourself? When you look in the mirror, are you the best friend to the one who is looking back? If you're in a good space with yourself, then outside relationships will take on lesser significance. Always remember you are the only person who has been with you since birth, and you will be the only person who will be with you at life's end. If you require any person, place, or thing to feel complete, you are in a state of codependency.

Wright

Then you have determined that the former would be codependency.

Deiser

Yes. If you are always looking outside yourself for completion, this is clearly codependency. It is a difficult and sad way to live, for everything outside of yourself is in a constant state of change. Start separating yourself from codependency by first changing yourself, as you are the only person you can effectively change. Recognize you are unique and an important player on this planet.

Down through history, the movers and the shakers of the world always recognized the importance of the individual, even the writers of the Declaration of Independence. First love yourself, and then you'll have love to give to others. This does not mean to become isolated, for obviously we will move in and out of relationships in the business world and in our personal lives. However, we'll be less dependent on what is outside and more dependent on what is inside.

Altman

So you are basically telling our audience to achieve a well-balanced life, that it isn't good to look on the outside of yourself, but you need to have some quiet time and go inside yourself. Is that correct?

Deiser

Yes. We don't take enough quiet time. We become dependent on everything outside of ourselves. The greatest support system we have is internal and is functioning very well without our help; for example, the heart is pumping, oxygen is being exchanged, food is being assimilated, toxins are being excreted—everything is on "automatic pilot." Science has proven that meditation or quiet time is of major importance. Recent research has determined there is a neural pathway in our brain that allows us to reach levels of thinking far beyond our normal finite thinking, but we must become quiet to reach it.

In the December 2001 *Readers Digest,* there is a report called "A Science of God." It proves what great minds have known for ages, that there is a level of thinking far beyond that of our earthly thinking. If you must become codependent, let it be on an inner level with the source that created you. Like the commercial once stated, "Try it; you'll like it."

Wright

Dr. Deiser, let me ask you a question. How often do people in your workshops admit to negative relationships with peers and family?

Deiser

Regretfully, very often, but it's not a surprise when you realize our formative years were controlled by so many outside of us. One of the things we do in our Science of Mind workshops and seminars is show the students that they can free themselves of the past. They can align themselves with universal truths, principles, and teachings that can set them apart from their history. Let go of the past. It serves no valid purpose to continue living there, particularly if it was unpleasant; rather, put your mind where your body is, right here, right now.

Wright

Do you think the reason people stay in bad relationships is because it is too much trouble to begin a new one? Is it too difficult for them?

Deiser

Not really. In my opinion, they stay in a bad relationship because the fear of change or the fear of being alone is greater than the abuse they are receiving in the current relationship. A perfect example is the battered spouse syndrome. The battered spouse will continually excuse the abuser rather than sever the relationship. Giving up anything is scary, but we have what it takes to do it if we make up our minds to do it. It is difficult, but it can be done.

Altman

Well, back to the prior question—is it possible to motivate others to action when many people are saying all motivation comes from within?

Deiser

Yes and no. My favorite saying is, "When the student is ready, the teacher appears."

Altman

What do you mean?

Deiser

It is a powerful statement. That is why many can't be motivated no matter what the outside stimulus is. No one can motivate you until you are open and willing to consider change. That's why external motivation so often fails. People go to thousands of lectures, seminars, and classes, yet rarely change. I resisted a great deal of good advice a major part of my life because I knew it all. I had some-one tell me at a time close to their death, "I tried so hard to help you, and you wouldn't let me. You are one of my greatest disap-pointments." I think that's what happens to many of us. Some of us just don't want to listen because we think we know it all.

Wright

Dr. Deiser, with our *Mission Possible!* talk show and book, we are trying to encourage people in our audience to be better, live better, and be more fulfilled by listening to the examples of our guests. Is there anything or anyone in your life who has made a difference for you and helped you to be a better person?

Deiser

Addressing the "anything," my answer is yes. I finally reached the point when all I had read, all I had listened to, all I had been taught seemingly made sense because I was finally ready to listen. I repeat: When the student is ready, the teacher appears. My teachers were many but I had to be ready to listen and consider change.

As to the "anyone," several people come to mind when I think of various critical times in my life. The birth of each of my five children drove me toward greater ambition and higher aspirations. My wife, Phyllis, is the wind beneath my wings. I am overjoyed to have a healthy codependence when it comes to her. Sharing life with her these twenty-one years has been fun. Then there are some of my teachers: Dr. Franklin Owen, D.C. (deceased), who introduced me to the chiropractic profession; Dr. Raymond Charles Barker of Religious Science, New York (deceased); and Dr. Eric Butterworth, Unity Church, New York, very much alive; Dr. Bill Taliafero, who continues to be a friend and supporter of my ministry; and two other current mentors and friends, Dr. Jay Scott Neal of Freemont, California, and Dr. Tom Costa of Palm Desert, California. Lastly and most important, I have never doubted my internal connection to a friendly and loving Creator. It has always been my number one reason to be better, to live better, and to be completely fulfilled.

Wright

What do you think makes up a great mentor? In other words, do these people seem to have characteristics that mentors as a whole have in common?

Deiser

Webster says a mentor is a wise, loyal advisor, teacher, or coach. In my opinion, great mentors choose to listen a lot and talk little. They teach by example and love what they are doing. They are willing to assist and support your dream instead of superimposing theirs on top of it. They are always ready to give you reasons why you could accomplish your dreams and goals, and the words "I can't" rarely enter their vocabulary. They have been and continue to be good friends and are available when needed. They consider being a mentor an honor, not a chore.

Altman

Erwin, there is a lot of fascination with the TV shows about being a survivor. What has been your greatest comeback from adversity?

Deiser

Several come to mind. (Did you notice there are always several?) One in particular is this: I was born blind in my right eye but was blessed to have a fully functioning left eye. Then at thirteen years of age, a cell of toxoplasmosis activated and I lost sight in my left eye. My parents, after consultation with the finest doctors in New York City, reached the conclusion that I would be sightless for the remainder of my life. After a short period of confusion and adaptation, I felt I could overcome this setback and also believed my sight would be restored. However, for approximately ten months I became totally dependent on my other senses to compensate for my loss of sight.

Not giving up during that time period was a major shift in my thinking, for prior to this episode I frequently gave up on anything that was a challenge. The strength of my faith and my willingness to accept my blindness is what I believe allowed the process to be reversed. My sight was restored after approximately one and a half years; and other than requiring glasses to adjust the left eye to 20/20, I could once again see. After the restoration of my sight, everything took on new significance. To this day, I can go into rapture over a rainbow. Nothing is ugly; if I can see it, it's beautiful. Everything took on new meaning, and I am grateful every day for the gift of my sight and the gift of my life.

Wright

Dr. Deiser, if you could have a platform and tell our audience something you believe would help or encourage them, what would you say?

Deiser

Be grateful for the gift of life, for it is a gift. You are so very special. No one has been designed exactly as you are. (If you have doubt, check your fingerprints; no two are alike.) There isn't anyone who has had your combination of experiences, and all of us on this magnificent planet are waiting for you to show your greatness. You will learn the lessons of why you were placed in the physical world, and you will always reap the reward of your choices. You were designed for success. To be a failure takes a lot of work, so why not choose to be successful? Live life today, for no one is promised tomorrow. Live the day in a way that will make you proud and will allow you to say, "I made a difference while I was here, and the world is a better place because I'm in it." Give yourself a hug, because you should be your own best friend. In times of crisis, remember that you are one with your Creator, and consider singing our Center's theme song, "Row, Row, Row Your Boat," for in its lyrics are contained some of the great mysteries of life. If you don't know the lyrics, find them.

Altman

Dr. Deiser, one quick question. I hear so many people saying they have come to a crossroad in their life. They don't know what to do next. They don't know whether to go right or left, or they don't know whether to give up their present vocation or project and go on to another one. What would be your advice?

Deiser

When you come to what you deem is a crossroad, become quiet. Take a time-out. Listen to your inner voice. Ask for help, and then just listen. The answers will come in many ways—sometimes immediately, sometimes a bit later. Be patient, be trusting; the answers will come if you're willing to listen. Also, check with your mentors. I'll end this talk the way I started: When the student is ready, the teacher appears. Are you ready?

Wright

I can see we're going to have to have another half-hour session with Dr. Erwin Deiser.

Deiser

I'm excited about life—what can I tell you?

Wright

Dr. Deiser, we really appreciate the time you have taken with us today. Alex and I certainly appreciate your being a guest on *Mission Possible!*.

Altman

We certainly do. You are so very interesting and motivational.

Wright

Today we have been talking to the Dr. Erwin Deiser, an ordained minister of Religious Science and the president of Have You Hugged Yourself Today. Thank you very much, Dr. Deiser.

Deiser

When I hang up, hug yourself. Love yourself, for you are the one you will be with the rest of your life.

Wright

Can I hug Alex instead?

Deiser

Go right ahead.

Wright

Thank you very much. My wife won't let me do it, but I will tell her you said it was okay.

Deiser

I am sure your wife hasn't any fear. You don't sound like a person who is concerned about that.

Altman

We enjoyed it, Dr. Deiser.

Deiser

Good bye, guys; it's been a pleasure. Joy in your life.

Rev. Dr. Erwin Deiser
Religious Science Pembroke Pines
12800 7th Court, G207
Pembroke Pines, FL 33027 USA
Telephone: 954.435.3980
ppcrs@aol.com
www.religioussciencepembroke.org

Chapter 11

Dr. Carole Lieberman

Dr. Lieberman is known nationally and internationally as a "media psychiatrist." She is also one of the most sought-after psychiatric script consultants in Hollywood, consulting with two top-rated daytime soap operas as well as hundreds of other television and film projects. Her work as a script consultant has garnered numerous awards.

The Interview

David E. Wright (Wright)

Today we're speaking with Dr. Carole Lieberman, known as the nation's preeminent authority on the psychology of showbiz. As an internationally known media psychiatrist, Dr. Lieberman has appeared on *Oprah, Sally Jesse Raphael, Geraldo, Larry King Live, Entertainment Tonight, Montel Williams, HardCopy, E!*, and a host of other respected television programs. Dr. Lieberman, to do justice to your biography and really tell our audience your credentials would take up the entire program. Let me simply welcome you to *Mission Possible!*.

Dr. Carole Lieberman (Lieberman)

Thank you.

Wright

Let me ask the first question, Dr. Lieberman. In my research, I found that you're a courageous and outspoken leader against violence in the media. How did you get involved in this problem?

Lieberman

When I was training to be a psychiatrist, which I did at NYU Belleview, I realized that so many of my patients were influenced by what they saw in the media. Whether it was a soap opera, a movie of the week, a film in the movie theater, music lyrics, or whatever, they were particularly influenced by scenes of violence to become more aggressive in their own lives. For example, little kids who were exposed to violent cartoons became very aggressive when they were at school, and everybody was wondering why. Or kids copied the specific kinds of violence that they saw in their favorite cartoons or shows.

When I was finished with my residency, I decided to come out to California, the entertainment capital of the world, and talk to all of the producers and writers, and explain to them just how much what they were putting on television and on films and in other media was affecting the psyches of the world. Of course, I was rather naïve, because I thought all that Hollywood was waiting for was a great psychiatrist to come and tell them what to do. Surely if they knew what they were making was hurting people, destroying their lives— not just in terms of violence, but in the choices they made, everything in their lives—if they knew how powerful what they were doing was, they would want to take steps to make sure it wasn't harming people.

The media affects every aspect of our lives, unconsciously. We can see it in the way people dress after a certain movie comes out, or in copying the styles of movie stars or favorite singers. We see it in a lot of different ways, but we don't want to accept the fact that it affects us as much as it does. Even though people pay millions of dollars to put commercials on for that very reason—to affect what we do (our behavior) and what we buy—those in the industry and even just regular people don't want to admit they can be that easily influenced, that their minds can be "taken over" so that they unconsciously reflect the opinions and ideas that they see in the media.

I came out here and tried to explain this to people, particularly regarding violence, because violence is obviously spreading violence. Violence is the most serious of these influences. To my surprise, people weren't looking to find out this information. In fact, the information was very disturbing to them; they didn't want to feel as though they had that much power, because they didn't really know how to use it.

Wright

What do you say to those people who, on the other side of the coin, say kids are acting out their frustrations and their anger and everything through fantasy; therefore, it doesn't happen in reality?

Lieberman

That isn't true. Particularly in recent years, parents are not as involved with their children as they should be. Parents are still trying to live out the dreams that they never managed to finish and are kind of ignoring their children more than they should—some more than others, obviously.

When children are feeling angry, they're feeling like they are being abused, they're being neglected, and they do have a lot of anger. I think kids today are growing up with more anger than ever before. The problem is that when they see stories in cartoons, in television live-action shows, and in video games, they find ways of expressing revenge. That's why we have all the school shootings. And that's why we have kids getting into all kinds of problems, killing their parents, killing other people, becoming more aggressive, hurting other people.

Alexandria Altman (Altman)

Let me read a quote from you and perhaps you can explain it: "Traces of media influence can be found in every aspect of our daily lives, secretly altering how we think and how we feel." Is that really true?

Lieberman

Yes, that's what I was talking about before. It's easy to see when a certain style of clothes becomes popular that is directly attributable to some song or movie or television show. But the more subtle kinds of things and ways that we're affected are not as obvious.

One thing, though . . . when there are copycat crimes with specific telltale signs that relate to a certain movie, at least it does prove that the media *is* influencing us. In other words, it's hard to disprove that influence, if someone carries out a crime in exactly the same way as in a movie they just saw, such as *Natural Born Killers*. *Natural Born Killers* is the best example, because there have been so many people who have gone on killing sprees in a twosome, acting the way the characters Mickey and Mallory did. Then at least it helps to convince people that we need to stop this.

I think the biggest example right now that we're seeing is terrorism. I do not think it is a coincidence that some of these terrorist acts look like they just came out of a movie. How many times did we see in movies the World Trade Center crashing or burning? There are stories about people receiving bioterrorism agents in the mail. All of these different things . . . it's really as if the terrorists have been, to some degree, influenced by American media. Although "officially" they are not allowed to watch some of these things, surely there has been an infiltration of American media into these countries, and certainly it has affected the terrorists. This is the biggest example of copycat virus that we have ever seen.

Altman

Carole, what do you think it is going to take to wake Hollywood up to start doing more positive things?

Lieberman

That's a good question. I have been trying to do that for years. I think two things. One is a lawsuit. I have been involved as an expert witness in cases where Hollywood is forced by a legal decision to take responsibility for their actions. The second is when they feel physically threatened themselves by something, such as AIDS.

Here's another example: Years back, when there was the Rodney King beating and violence was spreading all over Los Angeles, people in Beverly Hills were all of a sudden worried that it might affect them. These would be some of the same producers and directors who would have created some of the violent movies that people saw and that stirred people up. I'm not taking away from what the Rodney King incident was really about—obviously, racism—but whatever our issue is, we're all operating at a higher level of aggression. It's easier to find a solution to what's bothering us by our unconscious minds providing these scenarios of how to get revenge, what to do, how to be violent. Just like any one of us getting angry at someone taking our parking spot. Maybe ten years ago we wouldn't have been this aggressive had we not consumed all these lyrics, all these scenes of violence. It's affecting all of us, not just people who ultimately go out and kill.

One example of being an expert witness and effecting a change is defense psychiatrist for Jonathan Schmitz in the *Jenny Jones* talk show murder trial. What I testified about was what his psyche was like, which was a combination of his childhood plus being pushed over the edge by the *Jenny Jones* show, which had him on as a guest. That was the story where another man came on and "ambushed" him. The man announced he had a secret crush on Jon, and then three days later Jon killed him. But it was because Jon was in a psychotic state at that time, having been pushed over the edge and lied to by the *Jenny Jones* show and treated generally in all kinds of ways. It touched on things in his own life and pushed him over the edge.

I'm involved in a *Natural Born Killers* case and various other cases where, hopefully, a court will find that these people need to take responsibility for their actions. It basically comes down to this: Only when their lives are personally affected—whether it's because they're having to pay money or because their homes or children are being endangered—are they going to wake up. It's very sad.

I must say that I have had some successes. There have been some people who have become more responsible, but it's not the majority, unfortunately. A typical scenario would be this: Somebody writes or directs a hit movie, makes a lot of money, buys a big house, gets into a certain kind of lifestyle and doesn't want to lose it. They continue to go for things that they hope will bring them the money to maintain that lifestyle. Freud said it a hundred years ago: Sex and violence, or sex and aggression, are inborn drives, so what these movie makers do is put things on that are inborn instincts that excite people in a very pathological way. It used to be that sex was socialized into love. The sexual drive and the aggressive drive were socialized into competitiveness and ambition. There were good reasons why we had these drives. Then, through seeing all these media pictures that show distorted views and that over-excite, these drives become violent.

Wright

As a staff psychiatric script consultant on TV shows—I think you've had that role on shows like *The Young and the Restless* and *The Bold and the Beautiful*—were you able to better equip them to deal responsibly with tough issues such as child abuse, multiple personalities, mental retardation?

Lieberman

Yes, this is an example of people who really do take their role very responsibly. The Bells, who created and produced these two soap operas, are very concerned with how accurately they portray the storylines and how they will influence viewers. I've been working on staff with their shows—they are the only ones who have a psychiatrist on staff. I read every script and give some ideas and certainly say whether or not things are accurate psychologically—in other words, would people do these kinds of things in real life? Or, if there could be some kind of negative fall-out from showing something in a certain way, I explain what that is. The producers are very receptive. It's been a very positive experience. These are the two top-rated soaps, which shows that you can be responsible, be accurate, and still be tops. Just because you are going to be responsible doesn't mean that you are not going to be popular.

Wright

In our publishing company, one of our best sellers is a book on stalking, written from the point of view of the author who had been stalked for several years. I was surprised that we would sell so many books, and that people would have that much interest in the subject.

Lieberman

Yes, stalking actually has become quite a problem over the years. I relate it in part to the movie *Fatal Attraction,* because I really did see a turn, an increase, after that movie, of people who somehow felt it was okay to go after the person they supposedly loved—the person they were obsessed with, really. They kind of felt validated by seeing that movie—that was what Glenn Close's character did. The other thing is that because of the media taking over our lives so much, people are finding it harder to distinguish between what's appropriate in the media and what's appropriate in our real lives. There's sort of a blur.

Altman

Dr. Lieberman, going back to Charles Manson and the Sharon Tate murders, what is it that makes these kids think that Charles Manson and his followers are so cool?

Lieberman

Power. Because people who feel powerless—and certainly children and teenagers do, now more than ever . . . people who feel powerless want to connect with or idolize someone who is powerful. Even though Charles Manson is in prison, he managed to commit a crime that was celebrated; and now that people want fame so much these days, they are in awe of someone who could hold that much power. Even though it is sick power—not power that anybody is using for good—it still is something they wish they had.

Altman

Let's change the subject for a moment. I want to ask you about your book *Bad Boys: Why We Love Them, How to Live With Them, and When to Leave Them.* Why do women fall for men that misbehave?

Lieberman

I have about twelve different types of bad boys in my book. These are men who are cheaters, stalkers, men who lie and have all different kinds of problems, men who want to be taken care of, and men who use women. The reason women fall for each of these different types has to do with the relationship they had with their fathers, what kind of unfinished business there is.

For example, if a girl had a father who was a workaholic, and he was never really emotionally available; or parents who divorced, and the father didn't pay much attention to her after the divorce; or a father who beat his daughter—whatever happened, that will make the daughter want to find a man where she can live through the same kind of scenario and try to make it come out with a happier ending. Sometimes it's the same kind of man, sometimes it seems like the opposite, but it's to try to fix it—to prove to herself that her father really did love her—by making this man love her.

Wright

Dr. Lieberman, with our *Mission Possible!* talk show and book, we're trying to encourage people in our audience to be better, to live better, and to be more fulfilled by listening to the examples of our guests. Is there anything or anyone in your life who has made a real difference for you and helped you become a better person?

Lieberman

When I decided to be a doctor—I was around seven or eight—it was from reading about the first woman doctor in America who opened up a clinic and helped people. I wanted to be like that. And then when I got to be a teenager and started reading Freud, I felt that he was really right in the things that he said, and I sort of wanted to continue with that work.

Stories too—Gandhi is another example—of people who went up against the status quo, against what was easy to believe in, and had the courage to try to change things. Freud had to undergo a lot of criticism. People became ruffled by his ideas; they made them uncomfortable because they were so true. The first woman doctor had to undergo a lot of opposition, and certainly I have in my own life. Some of the things we've been talking about go up against the mainstream.

I recommend that people read books or find out about the lives of people who somehow had the courage to stand, even though it cost them and was a personal sacrifice to promote what they believed in.

Altman

Most people are fascinated with the new TV shows about being a survivor. What has been the greatest comeback you have made from adversity in your career or life?

Lieberman

I guess I've been through all kinds of things in my life: earthquakes, fires, being a single mother, and living in the Peruvian Amazon jungle. Some of these things I sought out myself, such as riding wild horses in the south of France and clinging on for dear life. These have been some personal challenges. Then careerwise, it's kind of what I was saying before. I believe strongly in the effect of media on people, yet I work as a guest and a host and an author and all different kinds of things in the entertainment industry. It's always a struggle to stand up for what I believe in, criticizing the people who need to be criticized for what they are doing, biting the hand that feeds me, in a way, yet at the same time wanting to be employed by them.

Wright

Dr. Lieberman, here is what an article in the *New York Post* had to say: "Dr. Carole Lieberman, a UCLA psychiatrist and former chair of the National Coalition on Television Violence, refers to video games as a new drug." Then I quote you directly: "I think it's worse than television violence because children are pushing the buttons themselves. They're getting rewarded for destroying people in a game." Now that's a grim thought.

Lieberman

Well, it's true. I was talking before about how we are born with a sexual and an aggressive drive, and what happens when people are exposed to media, particularly things like video games, where you get involved yourself in pushing the buttons and seeing the results of your own personal actions. This excites certain receptors, brain receptors, and makes people addicted to this violence, because they get a high from it.

You can watch kids in a video arcade and see their expressions and how they want to keep playing forever, because when they win, they get all these bells and whistles, which is a lot more than most of them get at home. So they are being rewarded, essentially, for destroying people and things. It's almost like a psychological experiment with rats—they are being rewarded for doing these kinds of things, so of course they are going to do them again.

Wright

I've read some research about extremely high eye and hand coordination in children. They don't just shoot these monsters; they get them right between the eyes.

Lieberman

Right. And they've shown, for example, in some of the high school shootings, that these kids were able to be so successful because of all their experience with video games.

Altman

Dr. Lieberman, if you could have a platform and tell our audience something that you believe would help or encourage them, what would you say?

Lieberman

In these days, when we are all trying to cope with the stress every day of knowing that there is terrorism going on in the world, I actually have set up something to help encourage people— a "terrorist stress line." I'll give you the number for that. It's 900.860.COPE. I talk about the warning signals of terrorist stress, give people solutions, and also give people meditations to listen to, to relax, and to meditate for world peace. It's a place to listen to other people's messages and to leave messages for other callers, and to find out how to help children cope with terrorism. I'm working on setting up a live line where every day people would be able to talk directly to me for an hour a day.

Wright

Well, this has been one of the fastest half hours of my life, and Alex and I appreciate you being with us on *Mission Possible!* today.

We have been speaking with Dr. Carole Lieberman, known as the nation's preeminent authority on the psychology of showbiz. Thank you so much, Dr. Lieberman.

Altman
Yes, thank you.

Dr. Carole Lieberman
www.drcarole.com

Chapter 12

Carol A. Price

Carol A. Price is an international speaker and author with a background in teaching, criminal investigation, medical practice management, emergency center management, and counseling strategies. She stresses "outcome management" as the tool to make life successful.

The Interview

David E. Wright (Wright)

We are talking today to Carol Price, a professional speaker, trainer, and author. Carol's most requested topics include "The Hero in All of Us," "The Platinum Rules of Customer Service," and "Communication in the Workplace." She is the co-author of *Two-Minute Miracles,* a book designed to build self-esteem for the rest of your life, and has published three stories in the *Chicken Soup for the Soul* series. Carol Price, welcome to *Mission Possible!*.

Carol Price (Price)

It is my pleasure; thank you.

Wright

Carol, in your book *Two-Minute Miracles* you state that we have a tendency to think that if we attain certain things—the next job level, the college degree, the three-car garage—we will be happy. You call it the "race and chase." Can you tell us a little about that?

Price

Sure. I think that we traditionally get involved in a race and chase without even knowing it. I think we do it from a young age. There is a great deal of research that shows that from the age of three or four, our children know what name brand of clothing they are supposed to be wearing. I taught first grade for many years, and it was fascinating to me that when the children came back from Christmas break, they would tell each other what they got for Christmas. They would name the toys and the clothes they received by name brands. If they did not get the best new toy, or the best name brand of clothing, someone would say to them, "I got the better one; I guess my mama loves me more than your mama loves you." So what happens is, those children, by the age of four or five, who want and now "need" to have the right name on their jeans, or the right toy in their bedroom, literally believe if they get it—the right toy or the right shirt—they will be a happier five-year-old.

If we thought this concept was only affecting children, it might not be such a big deal. But the dilemma is, it isn't only affecting children. In fact, it gets more sophisticated as we get more sophisticated. We truly have been taught and have bought into that if we live in the right neighborhood, it's going to make a difference. If we live closer to the water (and that's a big deal in beach communities), we will take time to walk the beach, which we think will make us happier. If we do take off those five pounds around our middle, we will be more attractive to the opposite gender and will find a mate. If we have the right position at the university, we will be listened to. If I get that next promotion, then I will be okay. If I go back and get a Ph.D., then I'm a better person. The issue is not that it will make me okay; the issue is, if I want the Ph.D., just get it! But if I really believe it will be the thing that makes me happy, then when I get it and I'm still not happy, I have more evidence of my lack of worth.

We chase it and we try to beat the neighbors to get it. That's the race part. I want it before my neighbors, classmates, relatives, or mates. I want to go to my twenty-fifth reunion saying, "Gee, look at me now; aren't you sorry you weren't my friend?" Yet when I get it, I am still the same person. The day after I win the lottery, I'm still the same person . . . richer, but still the same. The day after that new car is in my garage, I'm still the same person. So as I chase it, as I enter the race, the important piece is, I will never reach the finish line. As I chase that thing, there is always a newer, better, or, in my language, a "gooder" thing to try and get. The race never ends, and I keep on losing.

Wright

When you live in a society where everyone thinks that way, it's really difficult to change, isn't it?

Price

The problem is that we believe everybody thinks that way, but they don't. We certainly have an example right now if we look at New York. There were a lot of people who were coming down the stairs of a burning building who weren't thinking of a new car. If we are bright, if we are sensitive, if we can stay focused, we are going to recognize that as those folks came down and the firefighters went up, there were so many more important things than how close to the beach they were, or the hope that no one sees their old car. I think there has never been a better time to understand what really matters. I hope we never lose that lesson. A couple of exercises that I use in my book really allow people to recognize what ultimately matters. Then it's up to them to decide whether or not they keep or change their beliefs.

Wright

I remember several years ago my young son, who is a young man now, came to me to get money to purchase basketball shoes. So we went to the mall. I wanted to buy Converse, and he wanted another more popular brand.

Price

And a more expensive brand, I'm sure.

Wright

Converse was $26 and the other brand was $90. I gave him $26 plus tax and told him to satisfy his own identity crisis, so he cut yards, made the extra money, and bought the other brand.

Price

I don't know how much training you have in this area, but perhaps without knowing it, what you did was brilliant. If he wants the shoes and is willing to work for them, as your son did, there is no reason he shouldn't have them. If he "needs" the expensive shoes and we give them to him for his "needs," then we have done one of the most horrible things a parent can do. You were right to allow him to choose to work for what he wanted—not needed but wanted. That proves the point. When we want things, we can achieve them, but when we "need" things, that need can never be satisfied.

Wright

I appreciate that. Carol, I was interested in the concept that we could think of ourselves as a group of circles like a bull's-eye with five rings. Would you tell us what you mean by that?

Price

I like to use the image of a bull's-eye to make this point. If you actually envision that bull's-eye, you have five places you could aim an arrow. Those places represent the five basic relationship bases. We have to decide where we base each of our relationships with the rest of the world.

Envision the centermost circle. I call that the *soul relationship.* When we have a relationship with another person that is soul-based, it means we believe that we are one hundred percent equal to each other in that relationship. We believe that their needs are equal to ours . . . not better, not worse, but equal. We believe that their wants are equal to ours.

I use the example of Mother Teresa who caressed the face of a leper with the same dignity that she would shake the hand of a president. In her eyes, she truly believed that the leper had the same worth as a president. It made no difference what their respective roles were, what they were paid, or what they were not paid. By being soul-based, we believe and she believed that they are as important as we are. That belief then dictates what decisions we make with and about them. Very often you will see a parent who has a soul relationship with a child, and the interesting dynamic is that the child does not share that soul-based relationship back. Part of the beauty of having a soul-based relationship is that you do not have to have it reciprocated. So, David, if I believe that you and I are exactly equal, it makes no difference whether you agree or not. I am still going to have and act on that belief. My relationship, my kindness, my decency, my whatever with you is then predicated on my belief of our equality, and that indicates how I treat you.

The next level or ring is the *heart relationship*. A heart-level relationship means that whatever I have an abundance of, I will quite willingly give away. As an example, if I have a great deal of self-respect in my workplace because I do believe I am good for this workplace, I will treat my peers with respect. If I have a great deal of self-respect, I am willing to give it away. Conversely, if I'm terrified that you are going to see through my front, and you will then recognize that I am stupid or inept, then I won't treat you with respect because I have to compete with you. I have to put you down in a meeting so that I look okay, I think. When we are heart-based, we truly give away what we have an abundance of.

Wright

Are you talking about giving away emotionally or tangibly?

Price

Both. The CEO of an organization or the department head who believes that he has enough information and knowledge is willing to share that knowledge. The department head or CEO who is afraid or not sure of herself will not share knowledge or the power of that knowledge, because she is afraid you will have too much of it and show her up. She believes if she gives away her knowledge, someone else will then have more and be better than she. So heart-based relationships reflect when people know they are okay, and they consequentially treat others well. I know I have self-respect, so I will treat you with respect. In today's world, if we look to sports, Wayne Gretsky never cheated on the ice. He had too much respect for the game and the skill. And yet without naming names, you can look at some of the young competitors in every sport who will cheat every chance they get, because to them they believe they are more important than the actual game.

The third level or circle of the bull's-eye is *intuition*. Intuition is a marvelous base for a relationship. Intuition says, "I'm not going to think too hard. I'm just going to do what I feel I need to do. My gut tells me and I listen." Interestingly, in our world and culture, we know that women have a better sense of intuition than men do. That is because they need to have that innate relationship with a five-day-old baby who isn't talking much at that point.

Wright

I've never thought about it like that. I've always thought it was unfair.

Price

However, it does equal out. We as women have a better sense of it, but men are more willing to use it. In reality, in day-to-day activity, men do a better job with intuition than women do, because we as women second-guess when it comes to us. Not when it comes to our children—we have a gut feeling about a child in danger and we don't care how foolish we might appear. But if our gut tells us something about us, we are more willing to question or ignore it.

The fourth level of the bull's-eye circle is *action*. There are people who, if they say it, will do it. The common expression "they walk the talk" is accurate. That level of relationship guarantees you can bank on their word. If they say they're going to be there at two o'clock, unless they die they'll be there. It also means they won't put it out there if they will not support it. So in the work world, as a boss, when they say, "I will support what you do and help fix whatever needs fixing," you know they will not hang you out to dry. The action circle relationships are based on trust: What is meant is said, and what is said is meant.

The last circle or level is the *observation level*. This is the most frightening one. The observation base represents "I will do whatever I think will play well in Peoria." A teenager might say, "I'm not going to show up at school unless I have those $90 sports shoes." People with observation-based beliefs and behaviors must have the right clothes and must talk the right way. If someone is giving a teacher a rough time and that person is cool, then the observation-based teen must back up the jerk in class. So part of our culture's reality is that the observation-based relationship is often the base of many teenage friendships. They believe, "I have to see if I'm cool based on whether I think you think I'm cool." Then, "If you think I'm cool, I must be cool." Therefore, the teenager acts and feels cool. And it never ends.

We can have different levels of relationships with different people. That's typical. We act and feel one way when we like who we are in a setting or relationship. We act and think differently when we question our worth in a situation or relationship. The goal is to make a decision that directs my life. That decision in my personal, professional, or secret life, if I have one, becomes "Do I want my attention, energy, and behavior directed from the inside out or the outside in?" In other words, do I want to spend my time with this person concentrating on things like equality and faith and giving (soul, heart, intuition), or do I want to concentrate on surface issues, like how I look, act, or talk? It boils down to this: If I drive my relationships from the center of the bull's-eye (heart and soul) rather than from the outside of the bull's-eye (observation), my relationships are genuine, authentic, and can be counted on. If I don't make that conscious effort, I can trust others as much as they can trust me—and that's not much!

Wright

I've got a thirteen-year-old daughter, and a lot of the parents that I hang with treat their children as friends. They say they want to be cool in their child's eyes and really want their child to think they are friends. I tell them I don't need another short friend; I'm trying to build a vital human being here.

Price

Right. And when she becomes forty, then you have the luxury to think of her as a friend. My gosh, when she is thirteen she has all the friends she needs. What she really needs is someone showing her the way to be successful.

Wright

In your book you talk a lot about assessing your relationships, specifically, the nine types of relationships. Is this a part of that?

Price

It's in addition to it. There is actually a test in the book. The test is interesting, because a number of people who really believe they know themselves well take this test and are not very pleased. Let me just go through what the test looks like, and we will give our listeners fifteen seconds to make some decisions. Please imagine nine circles that are connected like a chain. In fact, I call it the "truth chain" exercise. I ask people to place a name inside each link. They are given a description next to each link describing a relationship. The one rule that stays constant is that a name can only be used one time, so you need to carefully decide where each person best fits. Let's take the test.

The first link is represented by a person who has respected me better than anyone else ever has.

The second link is a person in my life who recognizes my value better than anyone else ever has.

The third link is a person who has liked me more than anyone ever has.

The fourth link is a person who has responded to my needs better than anyone ever has.

Fifth is a person who sees my potential more than anyone ever has.

Sixth is a person who emulates me more than anyone ever has. That means they want to be like me. Perhaps they want to grow roses as well as I do, or they may want my attitude about life.

The seventh link is a person who supports me better than anyone else ever has. I don't mean monetarily; I mean when I mess something up, they walk that walk with me. That means they support me through the ordeal even if they hate what I have done.

The eighth link is someone in my life who supports me less than anyone ever has. These are the people who believe that my behavior is never fast enough, accurate enough, or good enough.

And the last circle or link is the person in my life who discounts me more than anyone ever has. This is the person who really believes I will never measure up no matter what I do, try, improve, or change.

When people take this test, I ask them to take two or three minutes to fill in all the links that they can. In addition, I tell them that the people they choose can be from childhood, adulthood and/or the present. Once they do the exercise, we look over the results. What they have written astounds a number of people. The purpose of this exercise is to discover the identity of our support. Essentially, we all have two different types of supporters—either they attach a string or a condition to that support, or they offer it freely.

We are looking to be able to distinguish who in our lives accepts us as we are, or who says, "I'm here for you if you walk, talk, act, or live a certain way." The last step in the exercise is to draw a line in the chain that separates the bottom two links from the top seven. If you will recall, the bottom two links were, "I'm not supported by . . ." and "I am discounted by. . . ." The top seven links represent the field from which you can pull your "unconditional support." In other words, these are the people who will accept you as you are. They will accept you without conditions.

Now here's the kicker, and this is the purpose of the test. How many people who take this test use their own name in one of the top seven links? The sad news is, not many. But the real sad news is the terminology, the actual words used in this exercise, words like "respected," "value recognized," "needs met," and "potential seen." We have been taught that those words, those concepts of support, are supposed to come from the outside, not the inside; from others, not from us. If we are living a life from the inside out—heart- and soul-based relationships—then we have a chance to see those words as "us-centered." In other words, if I believe I have worth, I have to be seeing some of those words coming from me to me.

The following numbers are astounding. Literally, out of thirty thousand people who took this quiz, only six percent of those people in the sample group put their name in any one of the top seven links. Let me make this uglier: ninety percent of that six percent put their name in the fourth link: "My needs are responded to by . . . . " Here is the key: There is no one who can respond to our needs better than we can. When we say it's our husband, wife, mother, father, best friend, and so forth, we are faced with the fact that if this husband or wife dies or leaves us, or if this best friend moves to Yakima, our needs then are no longer met.

Wright

One of the things that I liked about your book is that most of the books we've read down through the last three or four decades say to be introspective, to look within yourself, but they give no methodology or technique. That's a real problem.

I was interested in reading about your trip to the Berlin Wall. In the book, you said you felt an absolute need to go there. Tell us why.

Price

It was about three weeks before the Berlin Wall came down. I'm not into a lot of history because it doesn't seem as intense to me as the present. But when something is happening at this minute that will be written about, I get real excited. The reality is that the Berlin Wall represented much more than communism and the Free World and the Iron Curtain. I think it represented to me that no matter how long it takes, right will come out on top.

I did everything in my power to get there. I arrived the second day and went across the border to East Berlin and had the most amazing experience. When I crossed the "old" border, the guards, who had no idea what their future held, charged a fee for passage. They were taking money at Checkpoint Charlie as a hedge against unemployment, I presume. Once in East Berlin, the few people who were walking around looked gray. Their clothes were gray, their shoes were gray, and their expressions were gray. They all looked down as they walked; no one looked up. In contrast, the people who were coming across the border were looking up, and many would fall to the ground and actually kiss the ground they hadn't been able to touch for forty years. Many collapsed in tears.

Here is the amazing part. West Berlin at that time was much like New York City. The buildings were impressive, made of brass and glass and marble. The shopping was upscale. It was a lovely place, and because this was November, much of the Christmas spirit was on display. We went into a department store and happened into the leather purse department. Many of the bags were stunning. Much Italian leather was on display. And then I saw her.

There was an East German woman, obvious because all her clothing was gray and topped by a gray babushka. She held the hand of a small girl (I assume her daughter), identically dressed in gray, right down to the babushka. She dropped her daughter's hand only to pick up a beautiful leather purse. She would touch it, rub her hand over it, and put it down, only to pick up another and repeat the process. After touching about twenty purses, she burst into tears and didn't move. The little girl just watched her mother. I went over to her and said, "Can we help you? Can we do something?"

My original thought is that she wanted a purse but didn't have the money to buy one. I was going to be this great American woman and buy a purse for a newly free East German mother of one. What she said to me took me by surprise. As she looked up she said, "I've waited over fifteen years to buy a pocketbook. . . ." That first part of her answer grabbed my gut. How often do we walk into some-place like Macy's and buy a purse, perhaps two, without a thought in the world? She continued as she pulled out a huge wad of money, ". . . And now that I have the money to buy one, I can't do it!" I asked her why. She said, "There are too many to choose from; I don't want to buy the wrong one." And with that she and her little girl left the store, without the purse, without making a decision.

We have so many choices. We don't often realize that our array of choices often limits us rather than empowers us. When we cut to the chase, cut to what we really want, the choices become fewer and more manageable. Our choices define us.

Wright

Carol, you stated that at the age of fourteen you wanted to die after having twenty-seven operations on your hands. That's a story in itself, and I hope you say something about that. With the help of a counselor, you used the ACT system. What is the ACT system?

Price

Let me give you a bit of background. At fourteen years old, after twenty-seven surgeries on my hands, I was embarrassed, ashamed, and never thought any boy would want to touch my hands. My prayer every night was, "Please, God, fix my hands or let me die." It was a sincere prayer. I wanted to wake up one morning and be as perfect as the women in movies and TV shows. My mom was truly afraid for me. She was afraid I would never be okay. She dragged me—and I sincerely mean dragged, because I adamantly refused to go—to a counselor.

The counselor was a young man just out of school. He forced me in his office to literally create something called the ACT system. ACT stands for As Compared To. He challenged me to choose three things in my life that I never wanted to lose or be without—the three things that I hoped would never be taken from me in my lifetime. I wrote down those three things on a piece of paper. They were *walk, talk,* and *see.* At the age of fourteen that simple exercise had such a profound impact on my life that I later went out and bought a gold locket and engraved those three words on it. I wear that locket every day and every night of my life. It has never been off my neck, not one day, not one night.

I use the ACT system because whatever happens in my life, or in my day, I now have something to compare it to. If you hate my guts, if I lose a job, if my airplane is late, whatever the crisis at the time, I will actually touch the locket. My bargain with me (note, I did not say my bargain with God) is that I can and will handle whatever comes along, as I know the three sacred things are safe. That simple action with that profound meaning has gotten me through some amazing situations in my life.

Wright

Carol, with our *Mission Possible!* talk show and book, we are trying to encourage people in our audience to be better, live better, and be more fulfilled by listening to the examples of our guests. Is there anyone in your life who has made a difference for you and helped you become a better person, other than the counselor?

Price

My mother was a very strong woman and raised me with the help of her mother, my grandmother. There was not a dad in my life, unfortunately. She said two things that I have carried with me forever, and probably those two things have helped form a great part of who I am. The first is, "Everyone hurts!" The "everybody hurts" message is that when I think that I may be getting over on someone, I tend not to want to do that. As a kid, the message "You sure got them!" seemed sound. Now it seems nothing but hurtful. "Everybody hurts" means that as I act and do, I have to make a conscious decision. Am I adding to, neutralizing, or taking away some of the hurt that is affecting someone else?

The second thing that my mother said is—and this is probably my credo, if I have such a thing—"Are you smarter than the problem, or is the problem smarter than you?"

Wright

Sounds like a wise lady.

Price

Indeed so. I was very fortunate.

Wright

You mentioned God a few minutes ago. When you consider the choices you have made down through the years, has faith played an important role in your life?

Price

It has in an unconventional way. I never have questioned the existence of God. However, I've not formulated an absolute picture of him at this point. I've done some exploration and still have some confusion. I have no question that there is something so much bigger than I and much smarter. But the faith issue for me is that we are derivatives of that faith and that God. We have to have faith both ways. We have to have faith that God does exist and is looking out for us, and we have to have faith that God determined we were capable of running our own lives with the help of that faith. I believe it is intended that we have faith in both God and ourselves.

Wright

Most people are fascinated with the new TV shows about being a survivor. As a matter of fact, I saw a lady bob for apples two or three nights ago, on one of the survivor shows, into a tank of snakes for a million dollars. What has been the greatest comeback that you have made from adversity? Was it the fact that you were born with the problem with your hands?

Price

Probably. I've always said that whenever we have serious adversity in our lives, as children or adults, and if that adversity is visible, we either crawl under a rock and barely get by or we kick the hell out of that rock and claim our rightful lives. I believe that the privilege of walking the middle of the road evaporates when we have adversity. I think the idea that at birth I can be given an issue that will be with me forever only tends to exacerbate the fear or courage I develop in response to that issue. In facing adversity I have the right to achieve beyond what I have been given as a limit. But—and this is a big "but"—I have to go and stake that claim; it doesn't come cheaply.

Wright

By the way, I'd like to give a plug to *Two-Minute Miracles*. I don't plug a lot of books, but I sure would like to give the audience the opportunity to find out where they can buy it. Again, the title is *Two-Minute Miracles*. Is it sold in bookstores or on the Internet?

Price

We make it available on the Web site. We wanted to keep it in a close circle. The easiest place to get it is really just go to www.carolprice.com and follow the links.

Wright

If you could have a platform and tell our audience something you believe would help or encourage them, what would you say?

Price

I developed something about twenty years ago that I often leave my audiences with when I speak. It's called the Star Journal. I'd like to be known for that. I have a number of people who say I am known for that, so I believe it is working. The Star Journal is a way to reinforce for us and teach our children that we matter each and every day. Here is the process. You need to get some kind of a book. A beautiful journal works, but a legal pad works also. At the end of your day, every day, you write two reasons that the world is better off because you exist. Reflect back on the day. When you do this with children, use the words, "What have you done today that makes the world happier?" It's easier for small children to comprehend "happy" in this exercise.

This is not a gratitude journal. Those are wonderful, but this is different, and I think the difference is important. The entries in the Star Journal reaffirm that I have actively chosen to make a difference in my world. Now, with this night's writing, let me go back and assess my day and my actions.

One of the greatest errors we make is forgetting that those tiny decisions that we have made all day long define us. The Star Journal allows us, at the end of the day just before sleep, to write down, "I was kind today when the person at the drive-through was patently rude." We don't think of that as a big deal, but it is a big deal. So there are documentable reasons that the world is a better place because I exist. If we do that nightly writing, our behavior changes.

Wright

This has been a fast thirty minutes. We'll have to do this again, Carol.

Price

Wonderful!

Wright

We have been talking today to Carol Price, professional speaker, trainer, and author. She is the co-author of *Two-Minute Miracles,* a book I hope our audience will buy a copy of and learn from.

Carol, thank you so much for being on our program at *Mission Possible!*.

Price

It was an absolute pleasure. Thank you.

Carol A. Price
Telephone: 727.397.9111
Fax: 727.397.3661
cpl1beach@aol.com
www.carolprice.com

Soul - 13

Sexual Energy - 17
Spiritual Life - 18

(20) Feelings Sell

Fear
——————
24 (is)

32-33) ASK tough ?s

over 100
——————
11
16

69) TAke Action

76 - Challenges